WHAT PEOPLE SAY ABOUT
BREAKING INTO THE PLAY

'Breaking into the Playground' by ~~and Murdoch~~ of the most useful pieces of professional reading that I have ever came across. It is detailed, well written and includes an abundance of excellent ideas and lesson for all age groups. The author's knowledge and passion for outdoor learning is demonstrated through the practical advice and explanation provided in this book. Anyone who is venturing outdoors with their class and are looking to embed outdoor learning into their lessons should get their hands on a copy of this book. You will not be disappointed.

Alan Hepburn, Acting Depute Head Teacher, Kirklandpark Primary School, Strathaven

This is a great resource for teachers, practitioners and any childhood practice students who want to broaden their knowledge and understanding of outdoor learning in an easy to read guide. The practical lesson ideas separated into curricula areas provide clear guidance that can be used by both experienced and inexperienced practitioners alike and differentiated to suit the needs of all children.

Caroline Jarvis, Childhood Practice Lecturer West Lothian College

A comprehensive book to put Outdoor learning on the map in your school – easy sections to help with panning, great suggestions to enhance learning outdoors and useful research to help staff understand the significance and importance for learning.

Kate Ringrose, Outdoor learning and sustainability coordinator, British School of Brussels

A fantastic resource for schools! It is packed with great ideas and practical, encouraging lessons for teachers and it is a 'must' for any school looking to enhance their provision of outdoor learning. Many of the lessons require minimal fancy resources and teachers could just pick up this book and run with practically all of the lessons found in here.

Carol Guthrie, Lead Teacher in Outdoor Learning, Clydebank

I would recommend this book for anyone that wants to take a small step or large leap into outdoor learning. It is a clear, friendly and incredibly useful guide to taking ANY learning outdoors and even as an experienced outdoor professional, I will be referring to it regularly!

Becky McGugan, Outdoor Learning Lead, Bassett Green

I absolutely loved all of the ideas section and it was great how you presented them by curricular area and had options for both younger and older students. The calendar of ideas relating to events by month was also fantastic as schools can zoom in on the events they already participate in and enhance their celebrations with new activities.

I would happily recommend this book. It is an extremely practical guide on how outdoor learning can be embedded into your practice quickly and effectively. It offers a plethora of ideas to enhance learning across the curriculum, many of which I can't wait to try!

Kirsty Smith, Primary 2 Teacher Dunfermline (Fife)

I would recommend this to anyone that works with young people and wants to incorporate outdoor learning into their work or have a better understanding of how it can be embedded into the curriculum and their current work. Its not just suitable for formal education, informal education can use the sessions to engage with young people and increase not only young people's confidence but also their personal and social development by participating in the many examples given of outdoor sessions.

Outdoor learning can also be linked to the National Youth work outcomes and young people can experience resilience, manage relationships, create and apply their own learning styles and consider risk and make reasoned decisions. This book supports all staff working with young people to easily integrate outdoor learning into their work and not just use it as an add on.

Claire Kane- CLD worker, CLD Youth services
West Lothian Council

I would recommend this book and I feel that every mainstream setting should have at least one copy in their cpd area. I also feel a lot of Early Years Practitioners would find this useful at nursery.

So one copy for every school
Make your outdoor area really cool
This book is a great learning tool
Buy it now don't be a fool

Maryanne Neil, Early Years Practioner
Craighalbert Centre

BREAKING
INTO THE
PLAYGROUND

AN INTEGRATED APPROACH TO
CURRICULUM BASED OUTDOOR LEARNING
FOR CHILDREN AGED 3-12 YEARS OLD

First published by
Carol Murdoch
16 Craigs Court, Torphichen, West Lothian, EH48 4NU

www.loveoutdoorlearning.com

Photography ©canva or © Carol Murdoch, 2022

Published 2022

DISCLAIMER
The publisher and the author advise you to take full responsibility for your safety and know your limits and relevant medical information for all participating in the suggested lessons and activities.
Before practising the lessons and activities described in this book, be sure that your equipment is well maintained and do not take risks.

SPECIAL THANKS

I had a wonderful team of educators who provided feedback and helped me develop this into a brilliant working tool. Special thanks need to go to Donna Chalmers, Carol Guthrie, Natasha McBain, Maryanne Neil, Kirsty Smith, Isla Bowden, Yvonne McColm, Justine Page, Alan Hepburn, Caroline Jarvis, Claire Kane, Becky McGugan, Ingrid Bruce, Gillian Reynolds, Anne Leonardi, Hetna Shah, Kate Nicoll, Elizabeth Falconer, Kirsten Mack and Andrew Bagnell

And anyone else who kindly provided support, encouragement and feedback for me.

Your time means more to me than you will ever know!

DEDICATION:

A huge thank you to every school, teacher and pupil I have worked with. They have helped me create this wonderful book.

Diane, you are a wonderful friend and proofreader - thank you!

Ian, you are my rock.

And to you, as a teacher, I know how selective educators are when it comes to professional reading so I appreciate you taking the time to read this.

Thank you!

CONTENTS

Introduction 1

Kit 12

Planning & Recording 14

Logistics 20

Risk 26

Concrete Jungles 33

Calendar for the Year 42

Garden 51

Lessons and Activities 59

English and Literacy 60

Mathematics 74

Health and Wellbeing 84

Technology 96

Religious and Moral Education 110

Expressive Arts 120

Social Studies 128

Science 138

What Next 152

About The Author 156

Bibliography 158

Index 163

INTRODUCTION

A few years ago, I taught a young lad, we shall call him Thomas. Thomas was what we called a reluctant writer; in other words, he would not put pen to paper. He was around eight years old and was still reluctant to write even his name.

One Autumn day, I took my class, including Thomas, outdoors for our literacy lesson. It was one of those typical autumnal days; the sky was blue, the wind howling, a nip could be felt, and that smell of the colder season was in the air. You know the type, one minute you are wearing your sunglasses and the next your umbrella is up and there is a gorgeous rainbow.

The class had settled down to do their writing, and after a short time, young Thomas came over.

"Miss, miss, how do you spell excellent?"

I took a moment and took a gamble, asking Thomas to head back to his seat under his special tree and try to sound it out. Off he toddled, and I stood, quietly observing, ready to help if it was too much for him.

But Thomas surprised me. He sat quietly, focused, eg., eg, egsel, egselent. Now, he didn't spell it correctly. But he tried. This was a significant breakthrough; he had shown himself he could try and he could write.

Sometimes breaking out of the confines of the classroom is all that is needed. I just needed to keep the momentum going when we were back indoors.

WHAT IS OUTDOOR LEARNING?

This is a question I get asked a lot, is it gardening, forest school, natural art, PE outdoors or taking your jotters outside? Or is it in the approach like Froebel, Reggio or Montessori? It is all of that and more!

The English Outdoor Council explains outdoor learning:

"is a broad term that includes: outdoor play in the early years, school grounds projects, environmental education, recreational and adventure activities, personal and social development programmes, expeditions, team building, leadership training, management development, education for sustainability, adventure therapy … and more. Outdoor learning does not have a clearly defined boundary, but it does have a common core."

It is simply impossible for a teacher to deliver all of that. But what they can do is deliver the curriculum. Therefore, within this book, we will be thinking about curriculum based outdoor learning. This is when you put your everyday teaching at the heart of your outdoor lessons.

Marchant describes curriculum-based outdoor learning as "the opportunity for an integrated, cross-curricular approach to achieving education aims". Experience has shown me that the outdoors, even just the playground, provides a range of real-life learning experiences which naturally create cross-curricular links.

Sometimes these lessons are chalk, sometimes art, sometimes rockets and sometimes even jotters! The critical aspect is that the outdoor environment plays a key part in influencing the lesson. Simply put, being outdoors gives you something that indoors does not.

I am in Scotland, and part of the curriculum design here is the requirement to give children and young people a breadth of learning opportunities. Taking concepts outdoors helps us achieve this as it develops the learning and, more often than not, requires skills to be used within a real-life context or in a different way.

glishoutdoorcouncil.org. 2022. What is Outdoor Learning. [online] Available at:

Marchant, E., Todd, C., Cooksey, R., Dredge, S., Jones, H., Reynolds, D., Stratton, G., Dwyer, R., Lyons, R. and Brophy, S., 2019. Curriculum-based outdoor learning for children aged 9-11: A qualitative analysis of pupils' and teachers' views. PloS one, 14(5), p.e0212242. <https://www.englishoutdoorcouncil.org/what.is.outdoor.learning.html> [Accessed 5 January 2022].

EXPERIENCE IS KEY
CHOCOLATE TIME!

Join me in a wee experiment. Take a moment and write down the adjectives you associate with chocolate (or your preferred food type, you'll eat it in a moment).

Only after you have done this, go and eat a little of it.

Now repeat the first exercise. Write down the adjectives you associate with chocolate (or your selected food).

Do the words change? Have you more? Has the experience of eating chocolate impacted you?

There is a place for teaching the concepts we can cover indoors in the outdoor environment. The experience that the outdoors brings to it will impact the learning.

Just like having that chocolate impacted you, and your list has likely changed!

Experiential learning has been valued since the time of Aristotle. It still has a place today. And the outdoors is an excellent conduit for this.

Beames and Brown explain, "teaching in authentic settings can considerably increase the level of student engagement, as they begin to see how the concepts they are learning can be put to use in real-world contexts".

As long ago as 1993, Adams made it clear that school grounds can, and should, be a place for outdoor learning. However, it was also noted that we should be wary as these same areas are often neglected and taken for granted by educators. Despite Adams writing this nearly thirty years ago, I would suggest that we are often guilty of taking our school grounds for granted and not fully utilising them as a place of learning.

One of the first things I ask teachers is to head outside and explore the playground. You would be amazed at how often they will suddenly realise things have vanished or appeared!

So, get outdoors. Try and look at your space through fresh eyes. Looking at it from your classroom window does not count! Please do not take what is there for granted but instead reflect on how it can be used for learning.

Aristotle. (2000). Nicomachean ethics (R. Crisp, Trans). Cambridge: Cambridge University Press

Beames, S. and Brown, M., 2016. Adventurous learning: A pedagogy for a changing world. Routledge. Vancouver

Adams, E., 1993. School's out!: New initiatives for British school grounds. Children's Environments, pp.180-191. Vancouver

BUT WHY IS IT IMPORTANT?

We live in a country where children spend less time outdoors than prison inmates (Carrington). This is worrying as there is clear evidence that time outdoors has numerous benefits. These include

- improvement in enjoyment and engagement with learning
- increased concentration
- improved behaviour
- connection to nature
- enhanced social skills
- improvement to health and wellbeing
- increase in attainment

In short, outdoor learning can enrich learning, develop skills and improve health and wellbeing. So why is it not more widely utilised at all levels?

Marchant suggests this could be due to a range of barriers, including the difficulty to evidence work, safety concerns, resources and teacher confidence; all issues we aim to address within this book.

They also note that to embed curriculum-based outdoor learning fully, we require school inspectors to fully understand and acknowledge the benefits to children and prioritise this within visits. With recent announcements from Education Scotland and the Department for Education, we are hopeful that this change is happening.

I have spent my entire life around education, from working as a support staff to being a teacher and now an educational consultant. My dad was also a teacher; it really is in the blood!

We would discuss the latest educational innovations and how we were being told these were good for teachers throughout the years. And often, this was hogwash!

But outdoor learning is good for you and the children. Heading outdoors just three times a week for 15-20 minutes each time has been shown to

- Reduce stress, anxiety, blood pressure, heart rate and more.

- 97% of teachers say that outdoor learning is critical for children to reach their full potential.

- 88% of teachers say that they and the children are happier after time outdoors.

- 88% of teachers say that children are more engaged in learning when taking lessons outdoors.

I have spoken widely about suffering stress and anxiety when teaching. I do not say it lightly when I state that getting outdoors helped me be a better teacher.

The reason I use the curriculum based outdoor learning approach when working with schools is simple.

It builds on teachers' knowledge and makes this tool more accessible. This builds teachers confidence and makes them more likely to give it a go and embed outdoor learning.

We need to acknowledge that the vast majority of teachers have little to no training in outdoor learning, despite it being present within the policy context of UK education for several years now.

More promising is the increase in student teachers participating in outdoor learning programmes as part of their initial training education. However, these still often remain optional classes, which means many student teachers enter the classroom with little to no outdoor learning experience.

Mannion suggests that there needs to be more work completed to train and support teachers in implementing curriculum focused outdoor learning, and this should focus on all levels. This is why we look at differentiation carefully within our planning and support later in this book.

Christie, B., Beames, S., Higgins, P., Nicol, R. and Ross, H., 2014. Outdoor education provision in Scottish schools. Scottish Educational Review, 46(1), pp.48-64.

Mannion, G. and Lynch, J., 2015. The primacy of place in education in outdoor settings. In Routledge international handbook of outdoor studies (pp. 85-94). Routledge.

Nicol, R., Higgins, P., Ross, H. and Mannion, G., 2008. Outdoor education in Scotland: A summary of recent research. Scottish Natural Heritage.

'What people think, believe and feel affects how they behave' (Bandura, 1986). Bandura states that perceived self-efficacy and people's beliefs about their abilities will directly impact their performance.

I believed that I would not be a good outdoor teacher for a long time as I had real trouble trying to remember and identify my trees and plants. I grew up in an inner-city council scheme, not surrounded by nature.

I was not alone in feeling this way. Ofsted in 2004 found that lack of teachers' confidence meant they "did not fully exploit outdoor learning opportunities or seek to develop them further". More recent studies have also found that teacher confidence often confines them to the classroom, where they already feel like experts (Scott et al., 2013). This is still the picture I see when working with schools today.

Teachers know their curriculum; it is their bread and butter. If we can use that knowledge and integrate outdoor learning, it becomes a tool in the teachers kit box instead of an add-on. We all know there is no time for add ons!

Bandura, A., 1986. The explanatory and predictive scope of self-efficacy theory. Journal of social and clinical psychology, 4(3), pp.359-373.

Britain, G., 2008. Learning outside the classroom: How far should you go?. Ofsted.

Scott, G., Boyd, M. and Colquhoun, D., 2013. Changing spaces, changing relationships: the positive impact. Journal of Outdoor and Environmental Education, 17(1), pp.47-53. Vancouver

WATCH YOUR LANGUAGE - GAINING PARENT SUPPORT

To properly embed outdoor learning, we do need support from parents. An easy way to start getting this, and help them realise it is not simply playing but is learning, is through sharing our lessons on the school social media accounts.

But there is something I often see schools doing, and it can lead to parents not understanding the benefits. Educators post great photos and talk about the activity instead of the learning.

If we were indoors using cubes for arrays in maths, we would not say we were using or playing with cubes to help us learn. We would say we were working on arrays.

Yet, we head outside and focus on the activity; we were completing a scavenger hunt looking for minibeasts, not that we were learning to identify minibeasts and understand preferred habitats.

So, my plea here is very simple, share what you are doing to help engage parents but be sure to watch your language!

KIT - MAKE YOUR LIFE SIMPLE

The first thing we suggest schools do is pull together kit bags for every classroom. These are simple, affordable and make life so much easier. As a teacher, there is nothing worse than going to umpteen cupboards to get your kit and finding things are not there.

You can see our kit on the next page, but you can also add a few things.

ID cards (the ones from the Field Studies Council are fab!) I love the ID guides as they are well written and contain a lot of information in a straightforward format.

A tarpaulin to sit on or stay dry under is also a good investment. Outdoor lessons do not need to be long, but it is nice to have a base if they are.

As a teacher, I kept my kit in a backpack, nice and simple. It always had a front pocket as that is where I kept the kid's medications. Having a set place meant everyone always knew where to grab it.

So, what do we keep in our kit?

Wool/ yarn – great for arts and crafts, measuring, marking off areas and more

Chalk – take your writing, letter formation, art, maths or more outdoors

Register – photograph your register and save the paper. If you are not allowed to do this, then use matte laminating sheets as you can write on these and then erase them to use again

Medications – I often kept these in the front pocket so children knew where to find them or had older children take care of their own medications

Phone – it lets you contact the school and them contact you

Camera – great for gathering evidence

Measuring tape (10m and sewing kit size)- handy for maths and more

Mini first aid kit – you never know when you will need it

Small ball – turn-taking or games

Electronic whistle - great for pulling kids back together and means you do not need to worry about anyone else using it (I cannot whistle, if you can, you may not need this!)

PLANNING FOR OUTDOOR LEARNING

15 minutes

Just 15 minutes per week (to start at least)

That is how long we suggest your lessons are. So, right away you will realise that 15 minutes will not be a complete lesson. It is part of a lesson. It is integrated; it is not an add on.   It is simple, it is easy, and it reduces pressure.

The aim then is to raise it to three sessions per week, and they can stay as short as 15 minutes. We are sure you will build your confidence and start delivering longer lessons.

The easy way to include these is before or after breaks outdoors. That way, the children can either head out early or stay out, and you do not have extra transition times.

The way I would plan for outdoor learning was very simple. I would plan my week, not even thinking about the outdoors but instead what learning I wanted to cover.

Once I knew what I was teaching, I would consider what would benefit from being outdoors. Sometimes it was the entire class, other times a station in my lesson, whatever worked for that day.

This approach ensures that outdoor learning is integrated.

Monday	Tuesday	Wednesday	Thursday	Friday
Maths recognising 2D shapes	Literacy Spelling magic e pattern	Maths Shape, exploring properties 2D	Literacy Extended descriptive, adjectives	Maths big maths assessment, mental maths
Literacy Reading groups and creating blurbs	Maths word problems 4 functions	Literacy Writing using adjectives	Maths tessellation	Literacy spelling and reading French
Science measuring weather	PE creating a dance sequence	RME Diwali, meaning and art	PE creating a dance sequence	Assembly

This is a very simple plan, but it is designed to explain how I approached the task.

I often hear schools saying they will add an outdoor learning section to their planning.

Do not do this.

All you need to do is draw a wee tree onto your plan to show what learning was delivered outdoors. Our lives as teachers are already busy enough without adding more work to them!

6 KEY PLANNING QUESTIONS

Which experiences will have more impact on learning if done outdoors?

How can learning outdoors enhance and deepen learning within curriculum areas?

Which experiences are best suited to a combination of indoor and outdoor learning?

How can learning indoors best be consolidated, progressed or enhanced using the outdoors?

What opportunities exist for linking learning across the curriculum?

What current affairs or events could help place learning in a more meaningful or interesting context for young people?

TIPS FOR STUDENTS

These tips are aimed at students, whether at college undertaking childcare or an access courses or at university undertaking teacher training. But, they will also be helpful to experienced teachers.

- Set the scene and the expectations. Make it clear that you are in a shared learning space, and you expect that same behaviour indoors as out.

- Take time to explore the school grounds and ask what areas are included. I have been in many schools with additional areas fenced off, but you can take lessons there.

- Start simple; you do not need to deliver an entire lesson outside; it can be part of a lesson. Could the outdoors provide an excellent hook to engage interest? Could it help develop skills? Could it be a space for groups rather than the whole class?

- Remember, you are still learning. Many experienced teachers find outdoor learning a challenge when they first start. It is ok if lessons do not go to plan; in my career as a teacher, they rarely did (indoors or out)!

- Be kind to yourself.

RECORDING LEARNING

Have you thought about how you will record learning?

Our approach is all about linking outdoor learning to the curriculum, so your normal jotters might be ok. But, there may be times you want to take them outside with you, and it might get wet or muddy.

Therefore, we suggest having outdoor records. There is nothing fancy about these at all. They will get wet and muddy, and that is ok. They are working documents and should not be pristine.

Depending on the age and stage of your children, you have different ways to approach this. You can have a jotter per child or a big outdoor record (like a floor book) per group or class. You know your kids; you know what will work.

But, what do you use them for?

In some lessons, you will want the children to write or draw outdoors.

But here is the crucial part. I get the kids and young people to spend just a few minutes noting down what they learned in every lesson.

They might be building dens but learning about teamwork or identifying birds but learning to use a guidebook or a myriad of other things. The point is to have them record what they learned. It can also be helpful to record what they enjoyed and how they can improve.

All of this combined means there is evidence of learning, progression and reflection in one wee jotter. It takes just a few minutes, but it does help.

If children are using a group or class record, you may give each child a different colour (for groups) or pop their name next to it (for classes), so you know who popped what down.

Remember, these records will get muddy, but that is part of the fun!

THE LOGISTICS OF OUTDOOR LEARNING

Teaching outdoors can be daunting if you have a challenging class or are new to outdoor learning. When I taught challenging classes, the change in environment would often see a change in behaviours. Children want to be outdoors and enjoy the change in environment, which can improve behaviour. However, there are a few strategies you can use to help you.

Position

Before I have the children positioned, I need to think about my position. I often found that ensuring I was facing the sun rather than the youngsters helped them focus. This is especially important if you are showing them something. This can also be true in high winds. Ensure you are the person facing the wind, and the children will focus more.

Grouping

How I ask children to stand in a group is often determined by the weather. If it is wet and windy, my voice will not carry as far, and children feel cold when standing still. Therefore, I would instruct the children to stand as penguins – huddled together to keep warm and close enough to hear.

My instruction might be "sticky elbows" if I wanted them close but not as tight, my instruction might be "Sticky elbows". All children stand in a circle with their elbows close to their sides but touching the person beside them. This gives a tight circle.

If I wanted to be a little more relaxed, I might give them an area to sit on; this can often be on a large tarpaulin or designated area.

How Long

Remember that you can spend as little or as much of a lesson outdoors as you feel comfortable. You do not need to teach the entire lesson outside!

Your Gut

I would also say always listen to your gut. You know your class. You know your capabilities. Listen to your gut and do what feels right, and it will work.

Teaching Space

Explain to the children that while you are outdoors, in their playground, it is the groups' teaching space during teaching time, and you expect the same behaviours as a classroom. It is such a simple distinction but can really help.

Attention

If the children are over a wide area, you need a clear strategy for bringing them back together as a group. For this, I had two strategies. I would either use a whistle or my voice. If it was a whistle, I might use an ocarina or duck whistle as they are a gentler sound. If I were using my voice, I would tell children that it was their job to pass the message on and get everyone across. Often, with a new class, the first time outside would see us practising this at the start of the first lesson outdoors.

What to Teach

For my first lesson outdoors, I would always select something simple, which would allow us to go over the behaviour expectations and practice coming together as a group. For me, this was often an art lesson using Andy Goldsworthy as a stimulus.

We must remember that not all children are familiar or comfortable being outdoors. Throughout my career, I have taught in severe and complex schools and mainstream and ASD bases. I found children in all settings who excelled in outdoor learning and others who were less keen on it.

Educators learn early on in their careers about Maslow's hierarchy of needs. The lower needs are all about feeling safe, secure and psychological needs. This can link to the Leuven scale.

1. Extremely low
A child is in obvious distress; this could be displayed as crying, tantrums, anger etc

2. Low
In a low state of emotional well-being, the child appears uncomfortable and unhappy. They may be shy or unwilling to participate, they may also use self-soothing gestures.

3. Moderate
The moderate stage is a neutral stage. Children are neither happy nor sad and maybe minimally engaging

4. High
This is a high rank, and children are observably happy children. They may be smiling, laughing and engaged on a deeper level and may even show curiosity.

5. Extremely high
In the final stage, a child is totally at ease, comfortable, and fully engaged.

Once we appreciate how children are feeling and recognise the signs, we can fully support them in their learning.

It can take time for children to build up their confidence outdoors. This is where short bursts of outdoor learning can be helpful as they build up their confidence.

But it is also where regularity is vital as, without it, children cannot develop a familiarity.

Often I will ask children to select a favourite spot, tree or area outside. This is their space.
Their own special place. They can return to it time and time again.

Do you remember Thomas from the start of the book? His safe space allowed him to try and push himself in a way that he could not do so in the classroom.

RISK ASSESSMENT

We want children to develop a sense of responsibility and ownership, yet how often do we afford opportunities for this? One way to do this regularly is to allow them to assess the playground/outdoor area you will be working in, identify any hazards or dangers and share them as a group.

Activity

Take the children outside and form a circle. Ask them what hazards might be out; they need to be aware of what they can do to mitigate that risk. Make a note of each hazard, as this will form the basis of your risk assessment. It is worth doing this outside as the children can look for the risks.

This list should include, but is not restricted to:
-Sharp/ prickly plants or other materials
-Anything poisonous, leaves, fungi, berries
-Branches, low or fallen
-Uneven or slippery ground -Insects, stings and bites
-General public -Roads -Dangerous litter, broken glass or needles etc
-Weather, sun, wind and rain can all play a part
-Water, rives, burns, canals, lochs etc
-Canopy, overhanging or dead branches

Remember, this is about teaching children how to manage risk. Therefore, for every risk they identify, ensure you discuss measures that can be taken to mitigate that risk. I did have one child once suggest we should prune every branch that was eye level to ensure children were not poked in the eyes, and we discussed why this wasn't the best idea but what else we could do.

Once you have your list, teach the children to assess the site or playground every time you go out. Give ownership to the children for this.

FIRES

We want children to learn to be safe around fire, and outdoor learning is an excellent tool for this. We even share a few ideas in the book about incorporating fire. But there are a few things you should be aware of.

DO NOT HAVE A FIRE WITHOUT INVESTIGATING THE FOLLOWING

First, please ensure you are appropriately trained. Different local authorities will require different training, so please check what you need.

Risk assessment is critical. Ensure this is fully undertaken and you are following all local authority guidance.

If you have been thoroughly trained/ deemed competent, have risked assessed and followed all guidelines, then ensure you follow fire safety rules considering space, position etc.

If you are cooking foraged items (nettles etc.), be aware of allergies, the children may not have consumed these before.

Experience has shown us that expectations and rules will vary across different authorities, so please ensure you undertake due diligence and investigate these thoroughly. This book in no way provides the training you require.

THIS IS OUR LEARNING SPACE

We have mentioned this already, but it is vital, so it is getting a section all to itself.

I have seen so many teachers take lessons outdoors, and the kids instantly disperse, start to play, stop listening, and it all descends into chaos.

It ends up feeling stressful for the teacher and the children.

But it does not need to be this way. There is a simple solution.

Talk to your class

Explain that the playground becomes your shared learning space when you are outdoors. The rules and expectations you have there are the same as indoors. Acknowledge that it is their space at break times, but the playground is an extension of your classroom when learning.

This may seem obvious to us as adults, but so are many other things that we need to remind children. Their minds are still forming, and experience plays a key part.

If you help the children understand what you expect, you are more likely to experience it.

CONCRETE JUNGLES

Since the 1800s, there has been much written regarding the setting for learning; we only need to look at Montessori to Emerson and Dewey, to name a few.

There is no doubt that "A natural space leads to richer imaginative play; increased physical activity; calmer, more focused play; and positive social interactions" (Nedovic, S. and Morrissey), but concrete can help us learn too.

I often go into schools, and I am told the concrete jungle is not inspiring and does not allow for outdoor learning. This is utter tosh! Yes, it makes outdoor learning more challenging.

We spend most of our time working within a concrete cube, and we make that stimulating and interesting.

Outdoor learning can, and should, happen regardless of the aesthetics of your grounds. Later in the book, there is even a chapter dedicated to concrete!

Concrete does not need to stop you. Make the mindset change and challenge yourself; you will be amazed at how easy outdoor learning can happen on concrete without a host of resources.

Dewey, J. (1938). Experience and education. New York: Macmillan.

Emerson, R.W. (1884). Lectures and biographical sketches. Boston/New York: Houghton, Mifflin, and Co.

Montessori, M. (1949). The absorbent mind. Adyar, India: The Theosophical Publishing House.

In addition to a range of lessons, concrete can also be excellent as you can paint it, which aids learning. Painted features in your playground can support learning at all ages and stages. We have seen schools access grants for these, particularly using Modern Foreign Language grants. Alphabets, 100 squares, multiplication grids etc can all support learning.

It can be as simple as identifying their letters and numbers or jumping up in sequences with the younger years. Even colour splodges have a place.

While these can all benefit children speaking their mother tongue, they also need these in the languages they learn.

Jumping in sequences can also be helpful for older children when working on times tables, though I didn't spot a grid to 100; these are easily created with chalk. We also know of schools that obtained funding through modern languages grants as children do need to learn numbers and alphabets in various languages.

The alphabet ladder can be used to support spelling or even literacy development. Can the children think of an adjective that they can see outdoors which matches each letter? Which letters have more adjectives? All you need is a piece of chalk, and a timer can add some fun to the activity.

Playground Markings
Playground markings are a great way to extend how these areas can be used. Some markings are very prescriptive and have one use only, but we would counsel you to get markings with open-ended outcomes.

- Consider hopscotch grids with no numbers

- 100 squares

- Alphabets

- Blank grids

And remember that these can all be used in a range of curricular areas, as well as modern languages!

The ideas for using playground markings really are endless, but here are a few ideas just to get you started.

100 square
Finding prime numbers
Spotting the times tables
Counting as you walk or jump
addition and take away sums

Empty hopscotch grids
These are magic, as you can use them for almost anything with just a piece of chalk.
Number sequences
Write down times tables sums
Write random numbers and can children say them
Draw in different emoji faces to help children identify and name emotions
Write in spelling words or patterns

Alphabets
The obvious thing here is to jump onto letters to spell words
Can you work along the alphabet and find adjectives for each letter
Can you find items in your playground for each letter

Creating sound maps
This is when the children sit and listen and creatively construct a map showing the sounds they hear and from where they came. It could be in words or images. Let them decide. It is a great way to tune in to their surroundings and works well as a mindfulness activity.

Develop children's use of adjectives.
A piece of chalk and let them go wild, writing adjectives next to or on corresponding objects. Then heading indoors and completing a piece of descriptive writing. It is a short, sharp but fun introduction to a lesson and helps children who need a little stimulus in their writing.

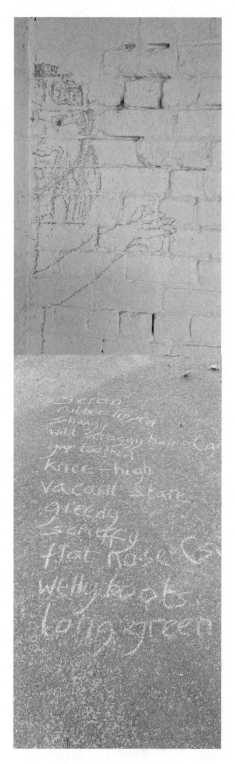

Use it as a creative stimulus.
What mythical creatures might they find within your school grounds? Can children describe them and their homes? Can they build a simple house with found objects or identify where the creature can live in the playground? What about writing stories about the creatures, diary entries or even cartoons? I have even had classes draw their cartoons with chalk outside, and the details were amazing! It is incredible how rich writing can be when the outdoors is a stimulus.

Measurement
Capacity
Give the children a range of containers, different sizes and shapes and explore the capacity. See if they can be placed into order, smallest to largest and then use water or sand to fill them up.

Distance
Can children mark how big a great white shark (3.4 - 4m long) is or how far the long jump record is (8.95m)? What about the length of an F1 car (varies but no longer than 360cm or wider than 200cm) and or measure a tree? Dinosaurs can be fun to measure as well. Basically, anything super big helps them understand.

Information Handling

Can you create Venn diagrams with found objects? This can be as simple or complex as is age and stage appropriate. The children can set their own categories and see if others can determine them.

There are so many ideas you can take outdoors without needing a field, trees or any greenery.

Big School Birdwatch (UK)
This is a great way to get out and do some real-life tally charts while you record your sightings. It also links to ICT when you upload results.

18th Winnie the Pooh Day
These stories are set in the woods and play traditional games, linking literacy with social studies.

21st Squirrel Appreciation Day
Can your class research squirrels?

29th Story Telling Week
Sharing stories outside speaks to our souls but also links to literacy. Check the Green Man lesson later in the book.

30th Draw a Dinosaur Day
Use our dinosaur measures lesson in the maths section to help discover how big they really were!

Chinese New Year
A new year is an excellent time for a reflective walk or discovering more about the animals.

7th Children's Mental Health Week
We have lessons to support mental health in the health and wellbeing section.

14th Valentines Day
Can you use loose materials in the playground to create hearts?

17th Random Act of Kindness Day
Can you do something to care for your local wildlife? It might be making bird feeders, planting trees, caring for a habitat.

26th Tell a Fairytale Day
What better day to look for fairies and fae in the playground? Link this to your literacy lessons by describing their homes and why they live there!

43

3rd World Book Day
Can you complete a scavenger hunt to find the textures on the Gruffalo?

11th Science Week (UK)
Can you fly a kite, spot a rocket, check out our science section for more ideas.

20th Equinox
A great time to explore why the length of a day varies, make sundials and learn about space.

21st World Poetry Day
Take your pen and pad out today and find somewhere to inspire a poem!

23rd World Meteorological Day
In our lessons, we help you make tools to measure the weather.

29th Dark Sky Week
Not one you can do at school but can you set some space themed homework?

Stress Awareness Month
Time outdoors is shown to decrease stress, anxiety, blood pressure, heart rate and more.

Move More Month
We have ideas in our lessons to help extend the learning that can be undertaken during the daily mile.

Community Garden Week
Is there a community garden you can offer a hand with? Or maybe start a school one?

23rd World Book Day
I love nothing more than packing a bag with a drink, some cake and a good book, then heading off to find a secret place to read!

23rd Skipping Day
There are so many skipping games; this is an excellent health and wellbeing day.

45

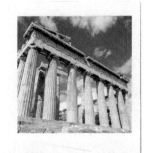

Walking Month
Have another peek at the daily mile ideas to see what else you can introduce

Share a Story Month
Can the children develop the green man story?

Local History Month
Head out and look for signs of history; it might be old houses, war memorials, battlegrounds, sculptures, buildings, or more.

5th Children's Book Week

6th Sun Awareness Week

7th Number Day
Take a number walk - you will be surprised how many places you spot them. You can use this to practice adding or multiplying as well.

21st World Meditation Day
More ideas for this in the pack.

23rd World Turtle Day

29th Children's Gardening Week

Pride Month

5th Environment Day
How can you help improve your local environment? Why not work with other classes to develop your grounds?

Gardening Week
Whether it is a pot plant, salad tub or a full veg patch, gardening is rewarding on so many levels.

Garden Wildlife Week

World Oceans Week

18th International Picnics Week
What better excuse for a picnic?

21st Equinox

23rd National Writing Day
Have a peek at our literacy lessons for some ideas

Children's Art Week

JULY, AUGUST, SEPTEMBER

July
17th Festival of Archaeology (UK)
Are there any archaeological sites that you can go and explore? Or invite an archaeologist to school.

August
21st World Photography Day
Have a peek at our stop motion lesson idea

30th Toasted Marshmallow Day
We love a campfire, do you?

September
3rd World Doodle Day
Grab your drawing pad and make doodles of what you spot today!

7th Youth Mental Health Day

17th Beach Clean (UK)

22nd Recycle Week

22nd Equinox

22nd World Car Free Day

4th World Animal Day
Sit quietly outdoors and see what you can spot... foxes, tapirs, butterflies? Research what you find.

5th World Space Week
Another week for homework! Can the children spot a planet, star and moon?

6th Badger Day
We love our fierce furry friends!

7th Poetry Day
Rabbie Burns provides a lesson idea in our literacy section.

9th Astronomy Day

10th World Mental Health Day
If your weather is turning colder or hotter, it can be tempting to stay inside more but make time to get out!

31st Halloween
Take a spooky walk or complete a spooky scavenger hunt.

November
5th Bonfire Night
Can you have a small campfire in your school? It is a great real life way to teach fire safety.

11th Remembrance Day

13th World Kindness Day

Book Week Scotland

30th St Andrew's Day
Can you use natural materials found outdoors and make a boat? It can be wee or big.

December
20th Festival of Winter Walks
Wrap up warm and head for a walk... or if it is your summer, enjoy a nighttime stroll.

21st Equinox

25th Christmas

31st Hogmanay
I always enjoy a walk to reflect on the year that has been

A SCHOOL GARDEN

We are often asked how to set up a school garden; indeed, helping every class play a part is something we discussed briefly. How do you ensure a progression for learning with the children?

We will share how you can create the garden and then discuss how to include it every year.

Before Designing, Consider
Identify a Location
Think about accessibility for all children and staff. Many factors should be taken into consideration to ensure all children can access and benefit from it. Distance to the garden, access, wide paths (at least 180cm wide will allow two wheelchairs to pass) and surfaces (surfaces enable wheelchair access, but a range of textured surfaces help children who are partially sighted navigate the garden). Other issues include access to water, storage of materials and tools, security etc., all play a part.

Check Plans
Find plans of the chosen site, available from the LEA, to determine whether there are any services underneath the surface or contaminants from previous land use that you should be aware of. If you are growing veg, which we recommend, you want to ensure there are no contaminants.

Risk Assessment and Safety

Look at legal, technical, safety guidelines and school policy documents as required and ensure any risk assessments are completed before work commences. There are likely other schools in your authority with gardens, so reach out to them and see what procedural hurdles they had to overcome. In my experience, schools with ASD bases and severe and complex needs often have the most incredible gardens, so it could be worth reaching out to them.

Incorporate and Share

Incorporating the garden into the school improvement plan is key. This is a straightforward way to ensure it is a priority for the year. But, at the end of the plan, ensure you keep going with it. This is the tricky bit! Also, shout about it to share the vision and get support.

Discover Skills

Like any big school project, it is always worth consulting with the parents, governors, PTA and the local community. Yes, Covid may make getting on the school grounds tricky, but could they offer advice over online meetings?

Maintenance

Who will care for the garden during the school holidays? Is there an after school/ holiday club that could jointly run it with you? What about the local community?

Designing

Survey

Once the site is identified, decide how big it is and investigate the soil, how much light there is, is there enough moisture, are there permanent features you need to work around, is there an entrance to it.

Establish the Purpose of the Garden

A wildlife garden is great for attracting the local wildlife and can be low maintenance but is it a project that could extend throughout the school? We find projects that involve the whole school tend to be those that grow produce or herbs. It could include herbs, vegetables, edible flowers, and some of these are even kind to local wildlife.

Decide on Shape and Position of Planting Beds

Narrow raised beds (no more than 120cm in width, or 60cm if only accessible from one side) is suitable for children as they can reach the middle for planting and weeding from both sides without compacting the soil. The height means children will limited mobility can access them. Raised beds can also be placed on concrete, widening the scope of where a garden could go.

Sustainability

Try to include a compost heap, and water butt is possible. You can always find compost bins being given away for free; ask your local community. You can even recycle old containers to create some beautiful pots.

Implementing your plan
Clear the Site
The first thing you need to do is clear the site of weeds and rubbish. Be careful if you choose to involve children at this stage; there may hidden dangers so ensure gloves are always worn.

Design the Garden
Try to involve the children as much as possible in the garden build as this helps them form a feeling of ownership and care towards it. Our projects showed that schools that experienced a high degree of vandalism found it decreased significantly when children felt ownership of the grounds and gardens.

Label Everything!
Even as experienced gardeners, we can forget this! Make sure you label everything in a large, easy-to-read lower case font. You may even want to use braille. Children enjoy making labels or signs.

Progression Through the Years

There are two stages to this: designing and creating the garden and maintaining it each year. We find that if each year group has a designated job that the children can aspire to each year, it helps maintain interest and sustainability of the project. Each assignment will need to be completed so that other year groups can conduct their roles.

Establishing a Garden

Primary 1/ Reception – Sowing! Can the younger years help by filling the planters with soil and work with older classes to sow the seeds?

Primary 2/ Year 1 – Signage! Can they create the signs and labels for the garden? These will likely need to be added as the year progresses.

Primary 3/ Year 2 – Survey! Can they consult the school in a survey to see what veg children like

Primary 4/ Year 3 – Research! Can they research what could be grown? There are so many different vegetables and varieties of each. Which will suit your garden?

Primary 5/ Year 4 – Planning! Can they survey and plan the site? This is a huge job but can be completed over a term.

Primary 6/ Year 5 – Fundraise! Can they write letters to businesses in the local community to help fundraise for the garden explaining the long term goal and benefits? It is much harder for a business to say no to a child.

Primary 7/ Year 6 – Design! Can the children design and build planters for the garden? This could be a great project with the local high school.

Ongoing Garden Maintenance
Primary 1/ Reception – Watering! Can the younger years water the garden regularly

Primary 2/ Year 1 – Signage! Continue to create the signs and labels for the garden; these will likely need to be added as the year progresses.

Primary 3 + 4/ / Year 2+3 – Weeding! This is an ongoing job that is better to do regularly. We have our weed finder sheet, which might help.

Primary 5/ Year 4 – Ordering and Sowing! Can they survey the school to see what veg children like and order the seeds for the year? Once they have the seeds, can they then sow them? It may be helpful to create a monthly timetable of what needs to be sown and when.

Primary 6/ Year 5 – Finance! You might decide to sell your veg to the school or community; if you do, can the children in p6 oversee this enterprise project? If you choose not to sell it, can they write letters to businesses in the local community to help fundraise for the garden explaining the long term goal and benefits? It is much harder for a business to say no to a child.

Primary 7/ Year 6 – Maintenance! Ongoing building of planters, stakes to support tall plants, pathways etc., all need to be taken care of. You might even choose to add planters or garden decorations/ art installations each year, which could be a high school project. Can the children do this?

LESSONS AND ACTIVITIES

As we go into the lessons and activities, it is important to note that outdoor lessons can often meaningfully cover a range of curricular areas. While we have popped these lessons into categories, this does not mean it is the only category the lesson falls into.

Each section is colour coded to make it easy to find, and the curricular links section is excellent for seeing which lessons fall under each curricular area.

English and Literacy

Mathematics and Numercay

Health and Wellbeing

Technology

Religious and Moral Education

Expressive Arts

Social Studies

Science

GREEN MAN STORY

There have been stories of green men told for centuries and across many countries. Whilst he can mean different things to different people, he often represents an environmental guardian and keeper of the forest. As teachers, we have a responsibility to teach sustainability. The green man can be a useful cross-curricular tool in exploring this.

We often tell a story when working with children in nursery all the way up to secondary; unfortunately, I do not know the origin of it nor the true version, yet children enjoy it, and it sparks their imagination.

The Green Man

The story goes...
Once upon a time, there lived a rich and vain young prince. He cared not for people or animals. Servants prepared his favourite foods each day. His every wish was granted.

One hot day, the young prince decided to ride his horse through the woods that were part of his kingdom, hunting small animals for fun. He raced over the woods and fields, scaring many creatures as he went. He thought that the woods and all its creatures belonged to him, and he could do as he pleased with them.

It was a hot day, and he needed to cool down. He came to a loch — a beautiful, clear, cool loch.

The young man began to remove all of his fine clothing. He laid his clothes neatly folded on an old log by the edge of the loch and tied his horse to a tree before jumping into the cool water.

While he was swimming and splashing away, a hand reached out from behind a tree and took his clothing and led his horse away. When the prince got out of the water, he discovered that he had nothing left to wear save a piece of rope. He took the rope and fastened some leaves to make a cover-up. He was a proud and vain prince. He could not go back to his home dressed like this, so instead, he hid.

The prince went looking for some shelter at night, and he stumbled into a cave. It was dark, and he was frightened, and he kept hearing animal noises all night. He didn't sleep much that night.

In the morning, when the daylight came, it was clear that someone had been living in that cave! He found some food, bedding and a container for water.

Over time, the prince settled into life in the cave. He fashioned a whole garment out of leaves. He ate from the land. He covered his hand with mud to prevent stings and reached into a beehive for honey to eat. He became acquainted with all the small woodland creatures, and he cared for them, helping them over swollen streams when heavy rains fell, ensuring they had food and water, and sheltering them in the cave on the chilly nights.

One day, whilst out walking, he heard the screams of some scared children. He raced towards the screams and discovered two small children trapped by a wild pig threatening to charge. When he had chased the pig off, they looked at him. He was covered head to toe with leaves and mud, with a wild-looking beard and hair.

"Are you the Green Man?" they asked.

"I guess I am," said the man, who no longer looked anything like a prince.

The children went back to the village and told their adults of the Green Man. As time passed, the villagers told their children a story about a Green Man who lived in the woods and cared for all of the tiny creatures. They said he even watched out for children in the woods. The villagers faithfully left out food on winter nights for the Green Man to eat.

Many years passed until one warm day, a hunting party came into the woods. A wealthy young man, a prince perhaps, became separated from his hunting group and decided to take a swim in the clear, cool loch. The Green Man hid behind a tree to watch. He took off his clothes, folded them, and left them under a tree.

The Green Man reached out a hand and took the clothes and the horse, leaving behind his garment of leaves and a coil of rope. He used a sharp stick to trim his hair and beard and rode into town, back to his parent's castle.

Some questions you could ask the children are

Who would be the green man now?

What does he need to protect?

Who looks after the forests now?

Why do they need looked after?

Why might so many cultures across the world have green man myths?

Some activities you could try are:

Create green men using clay or found materials

Create homes for animals

Build a den for the green man

HOW TO REMEMBER TALES

One issue I often encounter is teachers' reluctance to share stories like this or other folklore outside because they worry they will not remember all the story or confuse it.

This is where the rule of 5 comes in.

Read the story and then select just five key points in it. Try that now for the green man story.

Those key facts are all you need to remember. They are the important parts of the story; everything else is just fluff.

I must have retold this story hundreds of times now, for toddlers to adults, and every time I retell, it is slightly different. I often use many sensory links to help listeners feel their way into the story. I often use the location to connect the listeners.
There was one day where birds started squawking, so we included that.

But, when you start, remember your five things and go from there. Trust that your listener has no idea what's coming next!

WEE, SLEEKIT, COWRIN, TIM'ROUS BEASTIE

Having looked through a handful of Burn's poems, you soon realise the Ploughman Poet spent time outdoors. This shows in the observations he makes about nature in his poems. From Sweet Afton, where he writes about the river, birds, the hills and the winds to how he describes the stormy weather in O, Wert Thou in the Cauld Blast. Nature plays a huge part in his poems.

He sets the scene of a winters morning and the chill rather well! Indeed, being in Scotland in winter, I can appreciate the storms! The same is true for Up in the Early Morning. Then, of course, we have his description of the wee mouse in To A Mouse, written after he allegedly turned over their house with a plough.

Take a moment to read these, and you will understand that his affinity with the outdoors truly helped him write each poem. Yet, in school, writing lessons are so often indoors, with a jotter and pencil and no real exposure to the inspiration Burns enjoyed.
So, why not buck that trend and take the children outdoors to help inspire some fantastic writing?

Activity

Allow some time to explore some poems by Burns, looking at the simplicity and structure but also think about the contents and descriptions. This can be undertaken indoors or out.

Ask the children how they think Burns knew these things about nature? Did he learn it through books, paintings or through being in nature?

Now take the children outdoors and allow them time to sit and study nature. They may wish to make notes or sketches to prompt their thoughts. Allow time to create a poem.

Younger Children

Young children can try drawing the characters they hear about or see. Can they use description? Can they create a shorter poem?

Older Children

You can study some of the technical aspects of Burns and encourage children to include these to develop their writers craft.

SENSES POEMS

Using senses outside is a great way to help children tune in to nature. It opens up their creativity and aids their prose. A fantastic activity I enjoyed with all ages is the senses poem. It is simple. The poem itself is simple, it can be adapted, but there is beauty in simplicity. It encourages description and good use of adjectives. It can also be completed throughout each season, creating a changing wall display and an accurate understanding of how seasons, and our feelings with them, change.

Activity
Encourage children to consider their senses in turn. Talk about each and how we experience them. Then ask children to take their time to compose their poem. The last section, I feel, may consider touch but may also consider feelings. Either is ok. Finish by sharing.

Poem
I see...
I hear...
I smell...
I think...
I feel...

Younger Children
Younger children can draw a picture for each section. If they cannot write, they can still express themselves.

Older Children
Older children can be encouraged to use increasingly complex vocabulary, and each start can be a verse rather than a line.

The observant may have noted that the sense of taste is missing. It has been substituted for thinking.

The reason for this is simple.

I experienced far too many children who would start licking things in their playground to discover what they tasted like.

We do not want our children doing this, so it is easier and safer to substitute than have this risk.

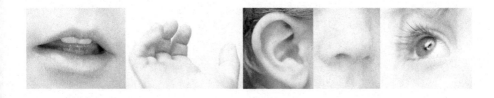

CREATIVE CREATURES

So many books are filled with mysterious creatures; they ignite the imagination and help develop a sense of curiosity about the world we live in.

Your class can create their own creatures to help develop their vocabularies. They can use leaves, flowers, twigs, stones, grass, anything really that you find outside!

This is a time to let imaginations run wild. Spend time creating the creature, think about where it might live, what it might eat, how it can move.

Throughout this activity, engage with your child. You can develop their use of adjectives by getting them to describe their monster.

Activity

Talk about characters the children know and recognise. Can they act out their creature?

Allow the children time to create their own creatures. The amount of time will vary depending on the age and stage. Ask what adjectives can be used when describing.

LITERACY

Tell the children to spend time reflecting on their character as they will follow this up with a writing Activity describing their character and its attributes.

Younger Children
Focus on words to do with colour, texture, size

Older Children
Can they use wow words? More complex describing words, elegant, curvaceous, ramshackle, ginormous etc

Next Steps
Can you create a longer text based on your character and use its description?

NATURAL LETTERS

Letter formation does not just need to be taught within the classroom with a pencil and paper. It can also be conducted in the playground, park or woods.

Finding loose materials is a fun and exciting activity. It encourages observation and builds a relationship with the natural environment.

It helps children understand how letters and words look. It is also great for displays and more – what better way to show work than with the lettering created and then photographed by your class!

Activity
Start by setting the expectations in terms of behaviour. Agree on what the children will create. Maybe just letters or whole words. Talk about materials. Let the children experiment. This could also be used as a station during literacy activities.

Younger Children
Create letters or their names

Older Children

Can create bigger and longer words. Have them focus on the materials used and why they are selected. Can you create an alphabet with letters that feature nature beginning with that letter? A = ash leaves, b = blades of grass, c = conkers and so on. This helps build up their natural world identification skills and their vocabulary.

Can your older children create an outdoor dictionary based on natural items or things found within the playground?

There is a beautiful book, Lost Words. This is filled with stunning poems with words lost from children's dictionaries because they did not use them. This book and your playground can work beautifully together to create poetry.

DINOSAUR MEASURES

In this activity, we are looking at the size of dinosaurs and their eggs. Having children measure the dinosaurs helps them understand just how big they are.

We do not have facts and figures for all the eggs as we could not obtain accurate data, or the eggs themselves have not been found as yet.

Younger Children
Please do not feel obliged to cover all of this with younger children; it will likely be information overload for them.

Older Children
Do as much as you feel they can cope with.

You can also use this as a measuring exercise eg
10cm = 1,000,000 years

Just make sure your space is big enough!

MATHEMATICS AND NUMERACY

1 step = (roughly) 1,00,000 years

1 step – the world we recognise and the history we learn about behind us!

3 steps – Homo Sapiens (us lot) appeared

5 steps – you could meet a mammoth for the first time

68 steps – lookout for tyrannosaurus

73 steps – lookout for a velociraptor

80 steps – have you spotted triceratops

91 steps – elasmosaurus is swimming around

153 steps – lookout for diplodocus

163 steps – check the skies for pterodactyloid

176 steps – Stegosaurus is now roaming the earth

208 steps – lookout for megalosaurus

230 steps – dinosaurs aren't around yet

SUNDIAL

Never eat sea weed...
that's the phrase I learned
as a kid to help me
remember the compass
points. Yet we were never
taken outside and shown
which way was north!

It would have been easy where I grew up as well; the
north was towards the river Forth! It took me a long time
to learn that the sun rises in the east. But this simple
activity could have changed that for me.

Activity
Each pair/ small group needs an area of 10-12cm squared.
Place your bottle down, and it can be worth carefully
drawing a circle around the bottle so if it is knocked over,
it can be placed back in the same spot. The bottle serves
as the sundial's gnomon and will cast a shadow.

Use a clock to time each hour and go outside to mark
the shadow on your sundial.

The shortest shadow should be at 12noon; mark this!
You should be able to mark each hour with chalk on the
ground as the sundial shadow moves.

Your numbers may not be equidistance; this is due to latitude and the distance from the equator (if you are using a stick instead of a bottle, you can tilt it a little north to take account of this)

Younger Children
This lesson is better suited for older children, but with younger children, you could explore shadows and how they change over the course of a day.

Older Children
Can they predict where the shadow of the bottle will fall ahead of time?

Next Steps
Can they do more work with time and direction?

SYMMETRY

Symmetry is often taught with mirrors and shapes on pieces of paper. Sometimes it is covered within art and with a self-portrait using half a face. Both are good, but why not use nature? Using a leaf encourages an eye for detail. They also look brilliant in frames or on a wall!

Activity
Ask children to find a leaf. It has to be a special leaf, a leaf they really like. It should be complete, not crumpled nor nibbled on. Once everyone has a leaf, give out pieces of paper or card. This can be indoors or out. You decide.

Ask children what they notice. Is their leaf the same on both sides? Are there differences? Carefully cut the leaf in half. This can be fiddly, so it is sometimes helpful to have some spare leaves handy, especially indoors.

Then set the children the task of drawing the missing part of the leaf. Remind them to press lightly with their pencil. The chances are they will need to rub parts out to redraw at times.

Younger Children
Just getting an accurate outline can be challenging.

Older Children
Should be encouraged to look at the tiny details within the leaf and try to include these

TALLY CHART BUGS

Whenever we talk about bugs, we are often met with teachers saying they are uncomfortable around bugs and would really rather not go near them. Hey, I used to be that teacher with a real phobia. Teaching minibeasts was a challenging term as I was constantly uncomfortable.

However, it is also our job to ensure these fears are not passed to our children or class.

So, the first thing I would say is if you do take the children out bug hunting, you do not need to touch any bugs yourself—remind your children that they do not need to touch them either. And, if they do touch them, they should be gentle.

Activity

Talk about bugs; what bugs might you find outdoors? This is an excellent way of developing vocabulary and checking for knowledge. You can then ask the children to draw pictures in their tally chart or create one using their ICT skills to make a table and print.

Then head out and look for the beasts. Where might they live? Can we be rough with their potential homes?

Ensure to go over clear handling rules.

MATHEMATICS AND NUMERACY

As you search, keep a tally of how many are discovered. Discuss the different types of habitats for various bugs. Can children work out why they prefer different spaces? Does the time of year or weather make a difference to what bugs you can find?

Younger Children
You can discuss
– How many legs do they have?
– Can you see the different parts of their body?
– How can you tell the difference between a millipede and a centipede?

Older Children
Can they use the results of this to create a bug home suitable for different types of bugs?

SCALE, RATIO AND MEASURE

I admit, as a teacher, I found these hard to teach meaningfully. They were always a bit samey in the textbooks and not much fun. Whilst we can sit and count squares, who enjoys that? And is it properly teaching children about the area and giving life skills, or is it more of an exercise to go through?

Activity
Use the school grounds to explore and create. Can children make a simple map of the school? Can they do it to scale?

Once you have a map, you can use that to create an orienteering course within the school grounds. It is a great way to help children learn and explore.

Younger Children
With younger children allow them to play with the concepts, they are not quite ready to fully explore them.

Older Children
With older children, let them explore. Can they use materials to recreate their school building? Is it roughly the right size? Are the different sections the correct size when compared to others? With even older children, can they measure the perimeter of the school building and create it to a set ratio?

MATHEMATICS AND NUMERACY

EXTENDING THE DAILY MILE

A simple way to support mental health is to get outdoors. Just being outdoors three times a week for as little as 20minutes a time is shown to improve mental health. Today we suggest some mindfulness walks you can do during your daily mile or set as homework tasks. These are aimed towards helping calm busy minds and help centre children.

Rainbow Walk

A very activity that even the youngest can enjoy is a rainbow walk. Older children can be asked to spot as many shades of a particular colour as possible. Ask them to keep an eye open for something which represents each colour of the rainbow. Depending on where you walk, the local habitat and the time of year, it may be difficult to spot every colour but try your best.

Silent Walk

Just let the world wash over you on this walk silently. Children might struggle with this one, so you can start short, just 60 seconds and build up. What did they notice on this walk that they had never noticed before? How did they feel on this walk?

HEALTH AND WELLBEING

Senses Walk

As you walk, take time to focus on each sense. Start by thinking about how your body feels. Are your feet hitting the ground hard or gliding with each step? Are your muscles tight? What are your arms doing? Try and focus, but once your mind wonders, move to the next sense. What can you hear? Is there a rustle in the leaves from the wind? A tip tapping of rain onto the pavement? Can you hear other people, traffic? Then we have smell; what smells are there? Can you smell exhaust fumes or the smell of snow coming? Let's not forget sight; what can you see? Try and take in every single little detail from around you. Taste is a trickier one; can you taste the air?

Slo Mo Walking

In this walk, we slow things right down. We take each step carefully, slowly, precisely. As we step, we think about what our bodies are doing, what muscles are working to help us balance? We are thinking about how these slow movements make the body feel. Try and breathe in and out in time with each step.

Each of these walks can be part of a walk or a full walk. It is up to you. As children grow more comfortable with mindful walking, they will be able to focus for extended periods.

Sensations

For this walk, you start low and work up. You start at the feet. How do your toes feel as you walk? Your feet, your heels? Take time as you walk to think about each part of your foot. Then move up to your ankles, your shins and calf muscles, your knees. How do they feel? Is there a rhythm happening in your body? Continue working up to your thighs, hips, back and so on. Once you get to your shoulders, work down your arms before finally working your way up to your neck, face and head. How does each part of the body feel when walking? Do they synchronise? What is the pattern of your walk?

WEEDS - FLOWERS IN THE WRONG PLACE

This lesson can be as simple as a scavenger hunt or the start of a PSE lesson that focuses on labels and their impact. We will focus on the latter but do feel free to use this simply as a scavenger hunt if you desire.

Head outdoors and allow them time to explore and find the weeds; some will likely be very familiar with and others less so. Some you will find where you live, and others you may not.

Once the children have had sufficient time to explore, it is time to talk.

Weed Identification

| Dandelion | Nettle | Chickweed | Hairy Bittercress |

| Goosegrass | Garlic Mustard | Ground Elder | Daisy |

Some Questions (select the appropriate ones for your age group)

- What did you think of the weeds?
- What did you like about the weeds?
- What did you dislike about the weeds?
- What does the word "weeds" mean to you?
- Is the word "weeds" a kind word?
- How could the weeds feel if they knew they were called weeds?
- What else could we call these plants?
- Do we call each other unkind names?
- How does it feel to call people unkind names?
- How does it feel to be called an unkind name?

Differentiation

This will vary depending on your class. As the teacher, you know them best and what they need. A class with a lot of bullying could use this lesson in-depth, whereas a class clicking along nicely may require less discussion.

EYES WIDE SHUT - BUILDING TRUST

Learning to trust others and how to handle trust given can take time to learn. This is especially true for those who have been bullied or faced difficult times. But we are going to explore trust in this activity!

Activity

This is such a simple activity and can genuinely be completed anywhere. Put children into groups of 2-3, or work 1to1 with a child. Explain that whilst one person is blindfolded or simply closes their eyes, the others lead them a trail. The leaders should be mindful. Their partners' safety is their responsibility. It can be helpful to demonstrate to a group of children how to safely guide someone else.

HEALTH AND WELLBEING

Can the children take turns in leading each other on a short trail? This can be around a playground, beach, woods, wherever works. How did it feel to be led? How did it feel to be the leader?

Younger Children
They may be less aware of any hazards, so ensure you talk through these. They may find it easier to hold their partner's hand whilst showing them the way. Alternatively, each holding a piece of string may also work.

Older Children
They should be more aware of any hazards and should therefore be able to take a slightly longer trail. They still need reminders about hazards. Can they guide only using their voice?

NEEDS AND WANTS

It can be hard to understand the difference between needs and wants in a consumer society. I want a cabin in the forest, but I just need shelter. I want a cheese platter but just need some food for sustenance.

Activity
If you have den building kits, set the children the challenge to create a space to keep their team warm and dry.

If you do not have den building kits, use a soft toy and set the same challenge. Can they create something to keep it warm and dry?

Aim to ensure all staff are hands off to let children explore. I purposefully do not give any more direction than this as it encourages problem solving. Well-meaning comments to support or give hints can detract from the learning here.

Once the den is built, let children carefully look at and explore the dens created by other teams. How do they differ? What aspects do they like? Can they improve theirs?

Then talk to the children about why a den is essential. What else besides shelter is essential? What is the difference between needs and wants?

Younger Children
I find that with this activity often, younger children look at life a little more simply and get the point but can struggle to create a den.

Older Children
As children age, often they lose confidence in problem solving, so some may require support.

Next Steps
This can be delivered over several sessions outdoors.

CLOUD GAZING

Cloud gazing. Clouds come in a variety of shapes and sizes. It is not only relaxing, but it can also aid learning from deep breathing and relaxation to literacy and more. For this card, we will look at how it can aid literacy.
 We can turn a humble cloud into a dragon or an apple, a hippopotamus or a tapir with our amazing imaginations! Encouraging children to describe them can help improve their writing when back indoors!

Activity
Start by allowing the children time to cloud gaze. They may be comfortable lying on their jackets, and indeed any children with hay fever will appreciate that. After a time, ask what they see.

Can they describe their cloud to their partner? You can model this behaviour by describing your cloud to your class as a teacher.

Allow time to practice before encouraging more complex descriptions or adjectives to be used. Again, you can model this.

Younger Children
Can they identify what the clouds remind them of? Can they describe them?

Older Children
Using adjectives is key here! Can they quickly sketch their chosen cloud then throw down as many adjectives as possible? This can be completed in a workbook or with chalk in the playground.

Next Steps
Let imaginations run wild! Can they create a story that happens in the clouds? It might be pirates riding the cloud waves, animals in the sky or a cloud fairy kingdom.

STOP MOTION LEGO MOVIE

Most children will have watched the Lego movie and will love the opportunity to create their own. This lesson has strong literacy and technology links, is outdoors, and encourages the children to look at their playground or local area totally differently!

Activity

Present the children with their groups Lego characters and set the challenge.

As a group, they need to develop an adventure for their character. It needs to have a beginning, middle and end.

It could be as simple as running across the football pitch as kids play or scaling the wall to look in the headteacher's window, letting the children's imaginations run free.

Show children how to set a scene and take a picture. Think about scale. Blades of grass are tiny to us but might be taller than your character.

Allow time to create a film. This may take more than one session outside.

Once the films are complete, children should share them with the class.

TECHNOLOGY

Younger Children
A simple 3-5 slide film would be sufficient.

Older Children
Ask them to think about how their character moves; minor changes in each slide can make a fantastic film.

Next Steps
Can children think of a story that features the outdoor environment more?

PHOTOGRAPHY AND HABITATS

Your playground or garden is bound to be home to countless animals; you just need to find them. This lesson will help your children learn about animals, habitats and develop their sense of place.

Activity
Set the children a challenge to discover what lives close by. They can start by suggesting what animals might live in the area. Then, they need to research the animals they come up with. What do their homes look like? Where might they live? What signs might be visible? Then it is time to get outside and start exploring. How many different animal homes can they find? Can they take a photograph of the home?

After their time outside, children should then come in and use ICT to create a factsheet on their animal(s). What their home looks like, with a photo, what signs did they need to look for, what does the animal need etc?

This is an excellent way of learning about biodiversity, even within concrete jungles! Think about what birds, mammals and insects might be there.

TECHNOLOGY

Younger Children
This lesson will be much slower paced and may take a few weeks to complete. There are so many skills included. Alternately, if you would like a more straightforward lesson, could you show them how to create a face file page in their jotters?

Older Children
They should work more independently and can potentially create a booklet with numerous animals in it.

WONDEROUS WEBS

Whether it is a fun STEM Halloween activity or linked to a habitat or minibeast project, spider webs are a fun and challenging craft to create. They are also easily adaptable for a range of ages and abilities.

Activity

This is a great STEM activity; it works so well for problem solving and requires a range of skills. Challenge the children to create a spider web using wool/ yarn/ string and natural materials. Some children might weave it through branches; others might lash branches together. What is key here is allowing children the time and space to try and try again. Often, it is natural as an adult to want to give suggestions and support, but the key here is space to problem solve.

Younger Children

With very young children, you may wish to use a paper plate rather than twigs, or maybe y shaped twigs if the children can find them. They may need to be shown how to tie a basic knot to start.

Older Children

Older children can cope with minimal support. Set their challenge and sit back. Watch. Listen. You could even set a group a task with a rope to make a giant web! It is a great way to learn how their minds work.

HOW WINDY IS IT?

A windy day isn't a day we want to be under trees, but that shouldn't stop us from getting outdoors! The Beaufort Scale makes assessing the wind speed really simple. In fact, I remember learning this back when I was around nine years old; thirty years on and I still remember it!

Activity
Ask the children what they know about wind and wind speed. Do they already appreciate that wind speed varies? How do they know how windy it is?

Introduce the children to the Beaufort Scale, invested in 1805 by the Irish hydrographer Francis Beaufort while serving with the Navy.

Ask the children to use this to assess the wind speed. Record and monitor it over time, does it change with the season?

Younger Children
Can they learn how to describe the winds using the correct vocabulary?

Older Children
Can they use the full grid independently? Can they update the effects for society today?

TECHNOLOGY

Scale	Description	MPH	Effects
0	Calm	0-1	Smoke rises vertically, trees are still
1	Light air	1-3	Smoke drifts
2	Light breeze	4-8	Leaves rustle, wind can be felt on the face
3	Gentle breeze	8-12	Twigs move
4	Moderate breeze	13-18	Leaves and small branches sway, litter and dust are lifted
5	Fresh breeze	18-24	Small trees sway
6	Strong breeze	25-31	Large branches sway
7	Moderate gale	32-38	Whole trees in motion
8	Fresh gale	39-46	Twigs break off trees
9	Strong gale	47-55	Branches break off trees
10	Whole gale	56-64	Trees uprooted
11	Storm	65-74	Widespread damage
12	Hurricane	75+	Devastation

STICKY BUILD

This is an excellent activity for developing problem solving and teamwork. Again, it is another lesson to be hands-off as the children will get there, regardless of age!

Activity
Challenge the children to create a free-standing tower using sticks only. They can work in small teams for this. Please encourage them to think about what needs to be done and give out jobs, so everyone is included. Older kids should be expected to do this themselves.

Younger Children
This is more about exploration for design and using materials; their towers may be small but encourage a problem-solving approach.

Older Children
Set clear rules; they will find any wiggle room. I usually say a free-standing tower using sticks only. Ask children to consider why they have selected some materials and not others. Allowing children additional materials like string may help them extend their tower. Have they worked out that triangles are the most robust shape? Can they build a tower taller than themselves?

STEM BOATS - ST ANDREW'S DAY

St Andrew's day is fast approaching, so we thought we would do a little research about him and see what lessons he inspired.

St Andrew was the brother of Peter, and both were fishermen. St Andrew is the patron saint of Fishermen, and here in Scotland, we have around 6,160 miles of coastline!

So to tie in St Andrew's, fishing and the sea we have the perfect activity!

Activity

Your challenge is to build a boat that floats. Provide children with a range of materials, from paper to plastic, lego or outdoor materials like twigs etc. Just use whatever you have handy. Once completed, create a water area, whether a tub, tray, or whatever works. Of course, if you are lucky enough to have a stream or body of water close by, that could be used too (make sure and collect all your boats after, we do not want to litter). If possible, allowing children to use trial and error during their build is helpful.

Have your children managed to build boats that can float?

Younger Children

With younger children just making a boat which floats can be challenge enough.

Older Children

You can enhance this challenge by solely using natural materials and string. It can be tricky to tie twigs together but is good fun. They can also be challenged to see which boat can carry the most weight without sinking. We love using glass counters for this.

MUSICAL WIND CHIMES

Making instruments can be simple and only use natural materials. This lesson can be entirely outdoors, or you can take the children inside to paint – though there is nothing to stop you from painting outdoors.

Activity

First, collect some sticks, finger width works well, and one a little longer and thicker for the main beam.

Then decide how to decorate them; you may leave them plain or paint patterns on them.

Once they are decorated and dried, you can use a little wool/ string/ yarn to tie onto the end. I wrapped it around 4 or 5 times before securing it.

Then, tie your individual sticks onto the main beam. You want them 2cm or so apart, so when the wind blows, they chime.

Tie a final piece of string on to hang your chimes up with.

Younger Children

They may find this very fiddly

Older Children

Encourage the use of knots

GOD'S EYE

God's Eye or Ojos de Dios are common in Spanish and South American countries. They are found within both Catholic and indigenous populations. Often, they reflect confidence in all-seeing Providence.

Activity
Explain to the children the belief behind this craft.
Get two roughly the same length and width sticks and hold them in a cross shape.

Using yarn, tie a noose knot and tighten it around the middle of the sticks to hold them in place.

Wind the yarn in figure eight around the centre, first from right to left diagonally, then from left to right.

Begin your first colour by weaving the yarn around the sticks. From the start, go over the top of the stick, wrap the yarn around it then move to the next step, always going over the top and wrapping around before moving to the next.

When you are ready to add a second colour, simply knot it onto the piece of yarn you are using and continue. Keep going until your eye is how you desire it to look. Ensure you loop and tie the last piece tightly.

RELIGIOUS AND MORAL EDUCATION

Younger Children
Younger children can struggle to get this started; an extra pair of hands or sellotape to start it may be helpful.

Older Children
Some older children find tying knots tricky but encourage independence.

Next Steps
Children can research God's eyes and learn more.

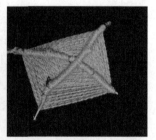

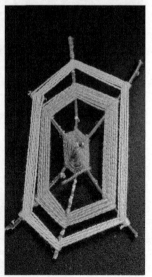

LABYRINTH

Like mandalas, labyrinths are an important tool to focus the mind and aid meditation. Creating a labyrinth helps children understand this religion and creates a sense of mindfulness, which is good for their mental health.

A labyrinth is simply a winding pattern that leads to the centre with no dead ends etc, as a maze would have.

Activity
Explain to children the significance of a labyrinth and see if any know what one is.
Demonstrate how to create one.
Allow children time to focus and create their own.
This should be an individual task.

Younger Children
Demonstrate how to create a labyrinth, explain it is like a path.

Older Children
Older children should be able to create a more complex labyrinth.

RANGOLI ART

During Diwali, the entrance to buildings is decorated with beautiful pieces of floor art, which can then be lit up with candles. Many teachers will encourage their classes to make clay diva candle holders, but nothing stops you from getting outside to create art.

Often, flour and rice are used to create patterns, but we can use chalk in schools.

Activity
Explain to children the significance of a Diwali and show some examples of Rangoli art before giving the children a chance to draw their design indoors.
As they only get one chance, remind them that they need to take their time when they are outside.
Begin by outlining in white.
Add colour.
Popular in Rangoli art are lotus flowers, symmetrical circular patterns or even depictions of Gods.

Younger Children
A simple shape or image can be a challenge.

Older Children
Encourage details and the use of colour. Older children can also be challenged to think about scale and make their art huge.

114

RELIGIOUS AND MORAL EDUCATION

MANDALAS

Having the time to absorb ourselves in a task fully helps us feel calm. It focuses on us and creates a sense of mindfulness.

A mandala is a spiritual and ritual symbol in the Indian religions of Hinduism and Buddhism, representing the universe. It is a series of circles growing in size from a central point. It can be completed with any age group and a range of abilities. This lesson can link to RME, maths, art and more. But it also encompasses several skills, including problem solving, exploration, decision making, teamwork and more.

Activity
Introduce the concept of mandalas; it can be worth doing so in class so you can show some examples on the smartboard. But if this is not possible, simply show the children how to start one. I always start with a central point, a leaf or stones and start creating circles radiating out from this point. I remind children they can use any materials found in the playground, but natural materials work better. Ask older children to think about patterns, textures and scale in theirs. Some children may create tiny mandalas, but others may create huge ones.
It always amazes me the amount of materials children find in a concrete playground, but if needed, chalks can also be available.

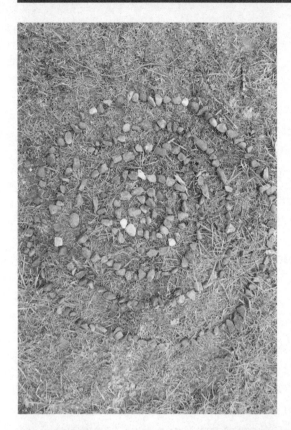

Younger Children
Can they create a circle using loose materials? Can they make each circle different?

Older Children
Allow freedom here, whilst I encourage use of circles, I have also seen some children create mandalas with other shapes as that is what they felt secure with.

CARING NATURE - BIRD FEEDER

As teachers and people, we are responsible for teaching children to care for their natural environment. Developing morals and values are intrinsic to religious and moral education. This should be explored through the general way you approach outdoor learning but can also be developed through simple activities.

Activity
Ask children who should care for the animals in the playground and why?
Explore their answers.
Give each child, or pairs of children, an apple that has been cored (older children can do this themselves with supervision)
Show them how to carefully pierce a hole into the apple and then push a seed into it.
Ask children to create patterns on their apples using seeds.

Collect two twigs per apple.
Leash twigs into a cross with a long piece of yarn.
Feed the yarn through
the apple, allowing the
apple to sit on the
sticks.
Use the yarn to tie to
a tree.

Younger Children
Give clear and concise instructions about being safe with a skewer. They will get fewer seeds into the apple.

Older Children
Ensure they are aware of safety with the skewer. Can they create patterns in the apple?

FIRE STORIES

Since the dawn of time, humans have communicated, learned and understood their world through stories. There is a part of us that still craves stories around the fire. Part of literacy is the enjoyment of texts. It is also listening. These can both be completed around a fire. Every school has its own rules about fire, but a small, controlled fire can be a way of pulling a class together. Of building relationships. Of developing that team. You can choose to read a story, tell a story or ask the children to share their stories. It is an excellent way to share work.

Activity
Start by setting the expectations in terms of fire safety. Then move on to talking and listening expectations. Once that is done, share a story. Finish by feeding back together around the fire.

Younger Children
They may be more inclined to listen to a story rather than tell one.

Older Children
Encourage older children to share a story they have created themselves.

EXPRESSIVE ARTS

COLOUR MATCHING

I am currently sitting in my office; there is a carpark ahead of me and some grass and trees to the side. If I glance at the flora, I could describe it as green. But on closer examination, it has so many greens, from the almost yellow-tinged green of dry grass to the bluey-green on the pine tree needles and a host more.
It is said that until we know a colour exists, we are blind to it. Imagine a world with no blue or purple? What about no reds or greens? We would be missing out. And that is not even thinking about shades – there is a reason there are so many in a Crayola pack!
Helping children explore colour helps their artistic abilities and supports their language development and understanding of the natural world.

Activity
An easy way to start this is a rainbow hunt. Can the children find all the colours in the rainbow?
You can then compare the colours, looking at the tonal differences.

The next challenge is how many different tones of each colour children find?

If children are collecting items, then talk to them about respecting nature. We need to leave some for everyone, including the birds and animals, to enjoy.

EXPRESSIVE ARTS

Younger Children
Simply starting at the primary and secondary colours is a good start (red, yellow, blue and purple, orange and green). Can they find lighter and darker shades?

Older Children
How many different shades of colour can they find?

CHLOROPHYLL ART

Chlorophyll is the green pigment found in plant leaves and is important for photosynthesis. Different leaves have varying success; try a few, but I often find spinach works well if you struggle.

Activity
In the middle of a piece of paper, sketch the trunk of a tree; it can be a very basic shape.

Fold the piece of paper in half with the trunk in the middle.

Place a few folded up leaves between the sheets where the leaves would go on your tree.

Use the metal spoon to press firmly on the leaves between the pages. If this is too hard, you can also ball up your leaves and use the scrunched balls to paint.

Younger Children
If younger children understand there is something within leaves that creates this, that is a good start.

Older Children
With older children, you can look into the science of this.

EXPRESSIVE ARTS

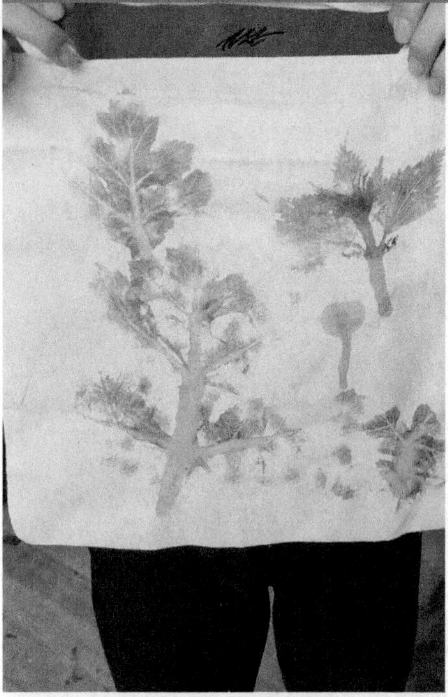

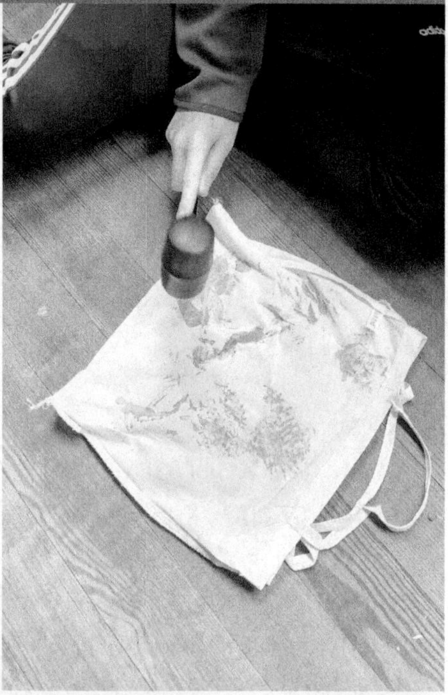

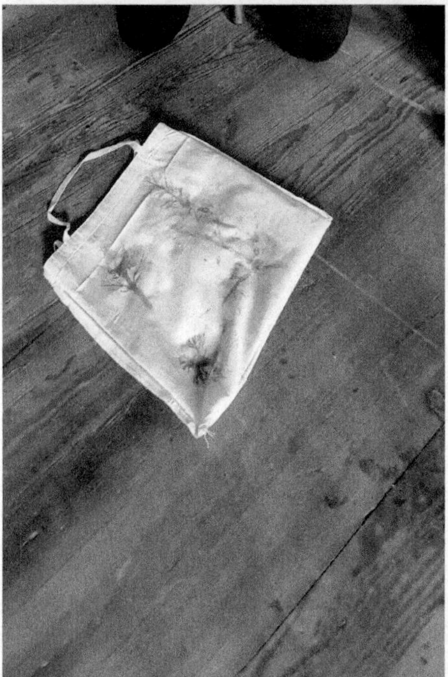

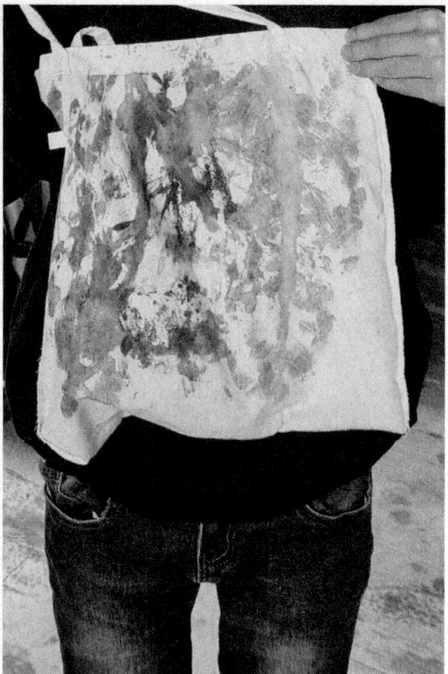

TWIGGY XYLOPHONE

This is a fun task that links both music and technology! Building musical instruments are fun and help children understand there is music everywhere. A xylophone is a really easy instrument to make outdoors and uses natural materials only.

Activity
To make a xylophone, you need two long branches and lots of sticks of varying lengths and thicknesses.

Lay the two long branches alongside each other; you will want one end to be close together and the opposite end a little further apart. This gives you a frame.

Find twigs long enough to be laid upon the frame.

The variety here will make the instrument more fun. For younger children, laying them in length order can be a challenge.

Once you have laid your sticks out, you have created your instrument. Find another stick to act as the beater.

Younger Children
Can they follow instructions step by step?

Older Children
Show older children a xylophone and let them problem solve how to make one in nature.

SHADOW HUNTERS

Shadows are everywhere, and the science of how they come to be is fun for children. But why not use them to help us create art?

Activity
One person has to stand still, with the sun behind them. The other person then draws on their outline. It could be with chalks or even just a paintbrush and water. Or you can do what we do and use natural  materials to create your artwork. The options are endless.

Younger Children
There isn't much differentiation required except detail; I would expect more from older children.

Older Children
There isn't much differentiation required except detail; I would expect more from older children.

Next Steps
Can children work out when the shadows will be longer/ shorter at different times of day, and why? Enjoying this activity at other times of day will help them explore that and link to the sun, solar system and beyond!

WE WILL REMEMBER

Every town, village and city have war memorials. They are a vital way of remembering the past. Once, the children in the class would have had real connections to the names on these memorials. But now, the link is often long forgotten. With the weakening of the link, the lessons of the past become dull and distant. However, we can bring that link to life. Take your class to the local war memorial. Talk to them about expected behaviour before you go. Collect the names of the men on the memorial.

Activity

Start by setting the expectations in terms of behaviour. Children should be reminded to be respectful at war memorials. You can talk about what they represent. This is worth doing before you go.

Move away from the memorial for your next step. Once there, ask each child to collect a few names from the memorial. Do they recognise any surnames? Could these people potentially have relatives still living in their area?

SOCIAL STUDIES

Younger Children
Recognising classmates names, either first or surnames can be a challenge.

Older Children
Once children have the names on the memorial, they can then begin investigating the people, their lives and where they lived. Old census records can be found online. What can children learn about their community in the past? (The census website can be a great help – https://ukcensusonline.com/

Next Steps
Matching names, investigating people and learning about the past is an excellent follow up here. Can you share this information with the local community?

OLD FASHIONED GAMES

So often these days children spend their time on screens or indoors and the games we played outdoors as children are fast becoming a din and distant memory, a thing of folklore. Yet these same games taught us about turn-taking, teamwork and cooperation. They taught us how to win with grace and lose with it as well.

Activity

Tig

There are so many types of tig, but a good old fashioned tig, with one or two chasers that swap every time someone new is caught, is a fun one.

Hide and seek

I love playing this with little ones as it really develops their body awareness, as they hide behind a pole, in full view of everyone! Remind older children about safety.

Team Catch

Set up a field, the children aim to get from one side to the other without being caught. Start with one or two catchers, and as each person is caught, they too become a catcher until there is a winner. Remind children how to safely tag, and no pulling is allowed.

SOCIAL STUDIES

Catch the flag
Split the children into two teams. They each get a different coloured flag. They then decide where in the playground to hide their banner. The aim is to grab the other teams flag. But if the opposite team tags them, they are out of the game. This is a great one for strategy and teamwork.

Catcher in the middle
Have the catcher stand in the middle of an area and close their eyes. The rest of the class is then to try and tag the catcher; the person who does it first is the winner. But, the catcher can open their eyes at any time and, whilst staying on the spot, turn 360 degrees; if they spot anyone, that person is out of the game. This goes on until someone catches the catcher or everyone is out. Set clear guidelines on how far children can go at the start of the game.

Younger Children
They should play most games but support by playing for shorter periods and ensuring simple instructions.

Older Children
Encourage older children to devise their own games once they are familiar with these.

HOUSE HUNTING

Understanding houses can help you understand how your local area has evolved over the years, but it also helps in story writing as it aids our vocabulary. Snow White and the 7 Dwarves would have been very different if it is set within a high rise flat, and can you imagine the three pigs building houses of concrete or moving into a semi-detached cottage, their poor neighbours!

Understanding housing in your area and country can also help you understand and compare housing in other countries, which can lead to you being able to explore how natural wealth is shared and compare populations between countries.

Activity

Take the children a walk. Ask them on the walk to identify different types of homes. There may be flats, bungalows, high rise buildings, tenements, detached cottages and more in your local area. What does this tell you about the area and the resources?

Are many of the homes built from the same materials? What is that material? Is it produced locally? Do the materials change depending on the age of the houses? Does the size of the homes correlate to their age?

Are there any unusual features? In Edinburgh's Old and New Town, you can notice many windows that have been bricked up due to taxes introduced at different times in history. Can the children re-create a version of your town?

It can be helpful to take a camera on this walk as it will allow you to record what you find and use this for reflection back at school.

Younger Children
Can they identify and name the different types of houses? Can they explain what materials the house is made of? You can always link this to the 3 Little Pigs.

Older Children
Can they use Google Maps to explore a different town or country and explore the similarities and differences? What does this tell you about the people that live in these places and how Do they live? What does it tell you about how natural are resources used?

HISTORY WALK

We are fortunate; history is literally on our doorstep. It doesn't matter if we live in a new town or an ancient village, an inner-city or historical city, how we shape the world and how it has been shaped; it is there for us to see. All we need to do is take a walk to discover it.

We can start by looking at the school itself. Is it an old school or a new one? Why was it built then? Does it relate to what was happening in your community? In my local area, we have new schools built when new housing areas were developed (many before the children were born but still feel new to us) and ancient schools in the community for over 100 years, established to support the children of miners etc.

But as you step outside the school groups, can you look at simple things like lampposts? Are they modern or vintage in design? Postboxes, where are they? What does this tell us? What about signs on buildings? Do we have ghost signs which nod to bygone days? As we explore more, we might start looking at buildings and houses. Often, pubs have a history if they are old. War memorials, or lack of them, tell us about an area. New build areas are unlikely to have one. How and where trees are planted can also give clues. Do they run in a line and are old? Could that be a boundary?

SOCIAL STUDIES

If we take the time and look, we suddenly realise that history truly is on our doorstep. We need to discover it.

Younger Children

For the youngest children, their walk is simply about identifying the things in their community that matter to them. It could be as simple as the school, shop, and home. But what landmarks do they pass on the way? Are there phone boxes, lamposts, trees etc., that all form part of their route? How often do children learn on their walk to school or nursery that they can run ahead to a specific landmark and then need to wait on their adult to catch up? That is part of their local history; it matters to them.

Middle Children

We can start focusing on the various things we find in the community and what they tell us for those in mid-school. If there is a phone box, why was there a phone box, what purpose it served, and why it is located? Remember, the children we teach now are used to wireless electricity and mobile phones. Some of the things within their community have no real meaning to them. In our communities, we can start discussing why we keep these items, which they may think of as being redundant. Can they begin finding evidence of how their community has changed over time? Look for new things and old ones.

Older Children

The oldest children can start examining the in-depth hows and whys; they can make links between what they see and how that shows the development of where they live. Even in new-build estates, you will have old parks and new parks, older houses, and new ones that tell the children? How does that mean their community has changed over time?

BREATHING LEAVES

Do plants and trees breathe? Here is a great but simple experiment to find out.

Photosynthesis can be a complex concept to understand; for young minds, plants and trees being alive can be hard to comprehend! So here is a simple experiment where you can see it with your own eyes!

Head outside and ask your children to collect a leaf. It is imperative that you collect a living leaf right off the tree. But equally, with older children, you can collect a dead leaf from the ground and see the difference. The larger the leaf, the easier it is to see the results.

Activity
Fill a bowl/ plastic cup with lukewarm water and pop your leaf in.

Pop a small rock on your leaf to ensure it stays submerged.

Now the hard part, pop it on a sunny window and wait a few hours.

When you check it in a few hours, you will see bubbles around the leaf and on the edges of the container.

Ask the children what would happen if they held their breath underwater and started to let the air out slowly.

What would they see? That is what is happening here! The leaf is still using the sunlight as part of the photosynthesis process (where leaves convert sunlight to energy).

As a leaf creates that energy, it needs to get rid of the items it no longer needs, so it will expel the extra oxygen during photosynthesis along with the water (this is called transpiration).

Younger Children
This is a great way to help younger children understand that plants and trees are living things.

Older Children
Can go on to learn about plant cells and more.

KEEPING IT CHILL (OR WARM!)

This is a simple experiment that is easy to set up. The aim is to discover which material is best for insulating an ice cube to prevent melting.

Activity
Set children a time to work together to decide how to insulate the ice cube. They can use a range of materials.

Once insulated, place their insulated cubes in a set location and do not move them.

Decide how regularly you will check your cubes (your weather, temperature etc. will determine this).
Which materials keep the cube from melting the longest?

Alternative
If it is really cold where you are, you could do the opposite and keep some water warm instead but be mindful of scalds and burns

SCIENCE

Younger Children
Exploring the terms temperature, weather, and using time accurately may be enough of a challenge for younger children.

Older Children
Can they use a broader range of materials? Can they explain why some work better than others? What may additional factors impact?

Next Steps
Can you write this experiment up correctly with your class? Writing a scientific report will provide you with solid literacy links.

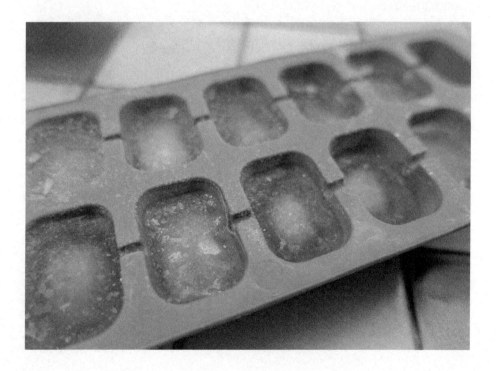

ROCKING ROCKETS

Rockets are fun, and they remind us that there is a lot more than just us! They encourage a sense of adventure and wonder. Your rocket can be as simple or as complicated as you like. They can be an old fairy bottle (those of us of a particular generation will remember those adverts) or can be made with Mentos (the sweets and cola explosion), whatever works for you. But, to keep it simple and mess-free, we have a straw rocket for you. How far can you blow it?

Kit List
Straws (you need 2, one wide one and a slimmer one that can fit inside the wider one)
Tape
Markers, pencils etc to colour your rocket
Scissors
Rocket – Rocket

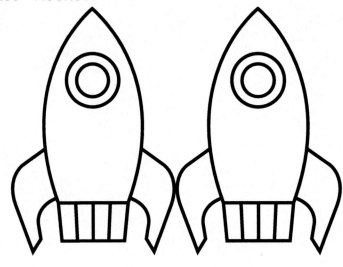

Instructions
Print, colour and cut out the rockets

Seal the end of the wide straw closed with tape and attach to your rocket with the closed end at the nose of your rocket

Slip the slimmer straw into the wide straw and you are ready to launch

Holding only the thin straw, blow into it and see how far your rocket flies!

Younger children
Can they describe the force used to make their rocket fly

Older Children
Does angle, wind direction or other factors affect how far your rocket flies? Can they make predictions on what angles etc will get the rocket to fly furthest?

SKELETON BONES

Did you know there are 206 bones in the human body? Although a child has 270!! The hands and feet combined contain more than half those bones. But why not get outside and get children to create skeletons!

Activity
Talk about the bones within the human body, can children guess how many there are? Can they name any?

Tell children they are to use twigs or other natural materials to create a skeleton. No twigs available? Simply ask a child to lay down and draw around them using chalk. Can children find things to act as bones or can they draw the main bones on?

Younger Children
This is a great way to help them learn the basics of the human body. Can they identify different parts?

Older children
This can be much more complicated. Can they recreate a skeleton that is close to being anatomically correct? Can they name or label the different parts?

SENSES

As adults, we take an understanding of the senses for granted. We know what our senses are and often, we expect children in the upper primary to know them as well. But it is amazing how many teenagers we have worked with who actually struggle to name the senses. Therefore, touching on the senses and doing a lesson or two on them with older children still has merit.

Activity
We have Senses Scavenger Hunts that are different levels for a wide range of children. Take them outside, any outdoor area will do, and allow time to explore.

Younger Children
Talk about the senses and help children understand each. Then select the appropriate level of the hunt for them. They may require some help with the written hunts.

Older Children
This can easily be linked to literacy. Can they create their own hunts, can it link to adjectives and descriptive writing? Do not assume they know the senses prior to the lesson. Give time to go over it.

Senses Scavenger Hunt

Hear
Something that makes a noise

See
Something with ore than 1 colour

Touch
Something that feels smooth

Smell
Somethingh that smells pleasant

Taste
Something an animal could eat

Senses Scavenger Hunt

Hear
Something crunchy
Something loud
Something squeaky

See

Something with ore than 1 colour
Something special
Something patterned

Touch
Something that feels smooth
Something warm
Something prickly

Smell
Somethingh that smells pleasant
Something which smells unpleasant

Taste
Something an animal could eat
Something a human could eat

Senses Scavenger Hunt

Hear
Something crunchy
Something loud
Something squeaky

See

Something with ore than 1 colour
Something special
Something patterned

Touch
Something that feels smooth
Something warm
Something prickly

Smell
Somethingh that smells pleasant
Something which smells unpleasant

Taste
Something an animal could eat
Something a human could eat

EGGY HEADS - ROAD SAFETY

This is a great experiment to remind them why wearing a helmet is important.

Use fresh eggs, do not boil them. You will be outdoors, so a bit of mess is ok; plus, it highlights the message. Ask the children in groups to use a range of materials to protect their egg. You will be dropping it from a height and seeing if they can help their egg survive. You can use newspaper, material, bubble wrap, whatever you have to hand, and no doubt copious amounts of sellotape once the children have "protected" their egg head outside with a rubbish bag or bin.

Once out, select an area where a little mess won't cause any issues. You can decide which height to drop the egg from; it could be shoulder height for the tallest person there or drop it from there if you have a raised area. The aim is to see what eggs remain intact.

You can then link this to what happens to children's heads should they come off their bikes; some protection is a good idea!

Younger Children

Can they work as a team with support?

Offer a selected range of materials.

You may need to support younger children.

Older Children

Can they hypothesise and work as a team independently?

Can they understand why some materials work better than others?

How does this translate to bike safety?

Offer a broader range of materials.

JUST A WEE CYNIC

Heels, pencil skirt, nails painted fortnightly and red lippy at the ready. If you were looking in the staff room, I was not the teacher who would jump out as an outdoor learning enthusiast.

In fact, on my first day of training in outdoor learning, I honestly did not want to be there… and that was not just because of the two buses to get home, and the wind and rain were howling. I honestly thought outdoor learning was yet another add on.

Being somewhat bullheaded, I went back to school and tried a lesson. Not because I was converted, but because I genuinely thought it would not work. How wrong I was.

I continued to teach outdoors when I moved to a severe and complex setting, then in an ASD base before heading back to the mainstream classroom.

Every change saw me convinced that it wouldn't work for the children in that setting. But every time I tried. And every time, it worked.

But outdoor learning was more than that to me.

Teaching is hard at the best of times. Did you know a teacher makes more decisions per minute than a brain surgeon? That is a heavy load to carry.

As a teacher, I struggled with my mental health; anxiety and depression were regular bedfellows. I often dismissed them as being part and parcel of losing my parents at a young age, but, with hindsight, working in such a demanding profession also played a role.

A recent study has come out by The Mental Health Foundation Scotland. It found that 51% of teachers state that the pressures of the profession have led them to develop mental health problems or exacerbated an existing problem.

Unfortunately, this is not a Scotland only issue. Studies completed by NASUWT across the UK found that 79% of teachers feel their profession has adversely impacted their mental health, with 23% of teachers requiring medication to help them cope.

Mental health may be one of the biggest silent stigmas within education, but it is widespread and only getting worse.

For me, outdoor learning was my escape, my chance to breathe. It was when I was most relaxed with my class.

Some days you do not want to be in that building. But, as Thomas showed us at the start of the book. Outdoor learning not only takes you out of the building but also helps support your physiological health. In basic words, it made me feel good. It also helped my class shine and make real progress.

Outdoor learning is not a silver bullet for education, but I genuinely believe it can make a real difference for everyone.

WHAT'S NEXT?

There are few developments in teaching that truly benefit staff, their health and wellbeing. Outdoor learning is shown time again to do so.

I founded Love Outdoor Learning back in 2017 to engage children outdoors while supporting families, teachers, schools and other educational settings.

For me as a teacher, the outdoors was my happy place. But I also saw it remove so many barriers to children's learning and reinvigorate staff.

I love it when people stop by to say hello or email me at carol@loveoutdoorlearning.com. Give me your feedback, ask your questions, share your goals! It genuinely makes my day when people reach out.

If you are looking for more, then why not head over to my website, www.loveoutdoorlearning.com
There is even some free content on there!

Why not join our group filled with educators from around the world
www.facebook.com/groups/breakingintotheplayground/

DOWNLOAD THE RESOURCES

If you would like to download the teaching resources from this pack please click on the QR code below. Once you join our mailing list we can send you the pack and keep you up to date with more lessons and ideas!

The A4 printable pack includes

The Greenman Story
The Senses Poem
Dinosaur Distances
Bugs Tally Chart
Weed Scavenger Hunt
Windy Anemometer
Rockets

And more!

ABOUT THE AUTHOR

Carol Murdoch is an educational consultant and primary school teacher who spent time working in a range of settings, including mainstream, ASD bases and severe and complex schools. She founded Love Outdoor Learning in 2017.

Carol has supported hundreds of teachers and thousands of children, helping them get outdoors.

Her approaches are simple and easy to integrate - she understands teachers are already overstretched, and there is no place for add ons!

Carol is an outdoor enthusiast who enjoys kayaking, paddleboard and even the odd outdoor swim. She will often be found in Mabel, her wee camper van, who she has been known to take when visiting schools across the UK!

You will find Love Outdoor Learning on Facebook, Twitter and Instagram and our website

FINAL THOUGHTS, QUIT THE CRIT...
AND STOP CHASING THE SHINY

As teachers, one of the first things we are taught to do is evaluate, or crit, our lessons and ourselves. How can we improve? What didn't go well? And we often forget to look at what did go well.

Then as our career proceeds, we have observations from our peers, management, the council, education inspectors, the parents crit us, the media crit us... it is relentless.

This impacts us negatively, both professionally and personally. It also stops us from seeing our progress.

I visit over 100 schools a year and talk to 100's more. The schools excelling with outdoor learning tell me that they are not doing enough. The schools who are struggling tell me the same.

Outdoor learning takes time to embed fully. We want to create something sustainable, and we do not want to burn staff out.

So take your time, take note of your progress and stop comparing yourself to others.

Just think, what would you tell a child in your class who was doing that?

BIBLIOGRAPHY

Adams, E., 1993. School's out!: New initiatives for British school grounds. Children's Environments, pp.180-191. Vancouver

Allison, P., & Telford, J. (2005). Turbulent times: Outdoor education in Great Britain 1993– 2003. Australian Journal of Outdoor Education, 9(2), 21–30.

Aristotle. (2000). Nicomachean ethics (R. Crisp, Trans). Cambridge: Cambridge University Press

Bandura, A., 1986. The explanatory and predictive scope of self-efficacy theory. Journal of social and clinical psychology, 4(3), pp.359-373.

Beames, S. and Brown, M., 2016. Adventurous learning: A pedagogy for a changing world. Routledge. Vancouver

Britain, G., 2008. Learning outside the classroom: How far should you go?. Ofsted.

Building your Curriculum: Outside and In (2011) Livingston: Education Scotland.

Care Inspectorate (2016) My World Outdoors

Carrington, D., 2022. Three-quarters of UK children spend less time outdoors than prison inmates – survey. The Guardian, [online] Available at: <https://www.theguardian.com/environment/2016/mar/25/three-quarters-of-uk-children-spend-less-time-outdoors-than-prison-inmates-survey> [Accessed 5 January 2022].

Christie, B., Beames, S., Higgins, P., Nicol, R. and Ross, H., 2014. Outdoor education provision in Scottish schools. Scottish Educational Review, 46(1), pp.48-64.

Curriculum for Excellence through Outdoor Learning(2011) Available at https://education.gov.scot/Documents/cfe-through-outdoor-learning.pdf

DCELLS (2008) Skills Framework for 3-19 year olds in Wales, Cardiff: Department for Children, Education, Lifelong Learning and Skills.

Department for Education (2014) Review of National Curriculum, 2011-14 Available at:http://www.education.gov.uk/schools/teachingandlearning/curriculum/nationalcurriculum

Department for Education and Skills 2006. Learning Outside the Classroom Manifesto. Available at:http://www.thegrowingschoolsgarden.org.uk/downloads/lotc-manifesto.pdf.

Dewey, J. (1938). Experience and education. New York: Macmillan.

Education Scotland (2015) How Good is Our School (4th Ed) Livingston: Education Scotland.

Education Scotland, 2020. Realising the ambition: Being Me. Livingston: Education Scotland.

Education.gov.scot. 2022. HM Inspectors of Education will undertake a phased return to scrutiny activities this academic year | News | News and events | Education Scotland. [online] Available at: <https://education.gov.scot/education-scotland/news-and-events/news/hm-inspectors-of-education-will-undertake-a-phased-return-to-scrutiny-activities-this-academic-year/> [Accessed 5 January 2022].

Emerson, R.W. (1884). Lectures and biographical sketches. Boston/New York: Houghton, Mifflin, and Co.

Inspiring Scotland (2016) Loose Parts Play: A Toolkit

Jenkins, E. and Swinnerton, B. (1998) Junior School Science Education in England and Wales Since 1900: From Steps to Stages, London and Portland, Or: Woburn Press.

Maller, C. and Townsend, M., 2006. Children's mental health and wellbeing and hands-on contact with nature. International journal of learning, 12(4), pp.359-372.

Mannion, G. and Lynch, J., 2015. The primacy of place in education in outdoor settings. In Routledge international handbook of outdoor studies (pp. 85-94). Routledge.

Marchant, E., Todd, C., Cooksey, R., Dredge, S., Jones, H., Reynolds, D., Stratton, G., Dwyer, R., Lyons, R. and Brophy, S., 2019. Curriculum-based outdoor learning for children aged 9-11: A qualitative analysis of pupils' and teachers' views. PloS one, 14(5), p.e0212242.

Marchant, E., Todd, C., Cooksey, R., Dredge, S., Jones, H., Reynolds, D., Stratton, G., Dwyer, R., Lyons, R. and Brophy, S., 2019. Curriculum-based outdoor learning for children aged 9-11: A qualitative analysis of pupils' and teachers' views. PloS one, 14(5), p.e0212242. <https://www.englishoutdoorcouncil.org/what.is.outdoor.learning.html> [Accessed 5 January 2022].

Montessori, M. (1949). The absorbent mind. Adyar, India: The Theosophical Publishing House.

Nicol, R., Higgins, P., Ross, H. and Mannion, G., 2008. Outdoor education in Scotland: A summary of recent research. Scottish Natural Heritage.

One Planet Working Group (2012) Learning for Sustainability Report. Edinburgh: The Scottish Government

Outdoor Learning – Practical Guidance for teachers and practitioners in Scotland (2011)

Quibell, T., Charlton, J. and Law, J., 2017. Wilderness Schooling: A controlled trial of the impact of an outdoor education programme on attainment outcomes in primary school pupils. British Educational Research Journal, 43(3), pp.572-587.

Rickinson, M., Clark, A., McLeod, S., Poulton, P. and Sargent, J., 2004. What on earth has research got to do with me?. Teacher development, 8(2-3), pp.201-220. Vancouver

Rose, J. (2009) Independent Review of the Primary National Curriculum. DCSF: London

Scott, G., Boyd, M. and Colquhoun, D., 2013. Changing spaces, changing relationships: the positive impact. Journal of Outdoor and Environmental Education, 17(1), pp.47-53. Vancouver

Scottish Government (2103) The Play Strategy. Edinburgh: The Scottish Government

Taking Learning Outdoors. Available at https://education.gov.scot/improvement/Documents/hwb24-ol-support.pdf

The Scottish Government (2012) Going Out There. Edinburgh: The Scottish Government

The Scottish Government (2017) A Blueprint for 2020: The Expansion of Early Learning and Childcare in Scotland: Quality Action Plan

The Scottish Government (2017) Space to Grow. Edinburgh: The Scottish Government

The Scottish Government (2018) Out to Play: Practical Guidance for Creating Outdoor Play Experiences in Early Learning and Childcare.Edinburgh: The Scottish Government

Waite, S. (2010) Losing our way?: declining outdoor opportunities for learning for children aged between 2 and 11. Journal of Adventure Education and Outdoor Learning. 10 (2), 111- 126.

Williams, A. & Wainwright, N. (2011) Changing Times for Outdoor Learning in Wales: Outdoor Learning Cards, Adventurous Activities and Physical Education. Horizons 56, winter 2011, pp.30-34

INDEX

A

adjectives 36, 38, 94-95
alphabet 36, 72-73
art - clay 64
art - drawing 78-79
art - natural 43

B

behaviour 20, 24-25, 30
benefits 1, 6-7, 152-153
body 144-145

C

colour 84, 122-123
concrete 33-41
creative writing 39, 70-71, 96-97
curriculum based 2, 6, 8, 16

D

daily mile 45, 46
den building 64, 92-92
Diwali 114-115
duration 22

E

emotions 89
experiential learning 4-5
experience 4

F

fire 28, 50, 120-121
forces 142-143

G

garden 45, 46, 47, 52-58
green man 60-64
groups 20-21

H

habitat 98-99
history - ancient 48
history - local 45, 128-129, 132-137
homes 132-137

I

imagination 94-96
information handling 41, 42, 80-81
insects 80-81, 100-101

K

kit 12-13

L

Leuven Scale 24-25
listening 38, 84

M

materials - properties 140-141

measure 40, 42, 74-75, 82

mental health - children 43, 45, 46

mental health - staff 45, 152

mindfulness 84-86, 94-95, 112-113, 116-117

minibeasts 80-81, 100-101

modern languages 34

months 42-50

music 108-109, 126

N

nature - caring for 43, 118-119

number sequences 36, 46

O

oceans 106-107

P

parental engagement 10

phonics 36, 72-73

photography 48, 96-99

physical education 45

planning 14-16

plants 88-89, 124-125, 138-139

playground 5

playground markings 34-37

poetry 44, 49, 66-69

R

ratio 92

recording learning 10, 18-19

relationships 90-91

risk 26-28

S

scale 82

science 44

senses 44, 68-69, 85, 146-149

space 44, 49, 76-77, 126, 142-143

STEM 50, 100-101, 104-107, 124-125, 138-139, 142-143, 150-151

stop motion 96-97

stories 42, 43, 44, 45, 46, 60-64

symmetry 78-79

T

time 76-77

traditional games 42, 45, 130-131

training 8-9

W

weather 44, 102-106

wildlife 49

WW1 + 2 128-129

Printed in Great Britain
by Amazon

24015649R00099